Quick & Easy
Stir-Fries

p

Contents

Introduction

Stir-frying is not only a healthy method of cooking your food but it also preserves the colour and enhances the flavour of the ingredients in the dish. In general, stir-fried food has been cooked quickly so that nutrients are retained and vegetables are kept crisp. Sauces may also be added later in the cooking process in order to create a wealth of Asian-influenced dishes with a multitude of flavours.

Oriental Cooking

Stir-frying originated in China hundreds of years ago and it is still the predominant way of cooking there. As a particularly economical way to prepare food — using only a short burst of heat requires only small amounts of fuel — this method quickly spread throughout Asia. In China it is called *Ch'au*, which means one or a number of ingredients are sliced thinly and cooked in a small amount of fat. In China they use bamboo

chopsticks to stir the food, so that it is evenly distributed and cooked throughout.

Although called different names throughout Asia, various forms of wok are used to stir-fry food. In India the *karahi* is used for stir-frying whilst the *wajan* in Indonesia is the favoured piece of equipment for creating quick stir-fried dishes. The selection of recipes in this book will introduce you to the richness of oriental cooking, from Thai-Style Stir-Fried Noodles to Chinese Pork Satay Stir-Fry.

Nutritious and Flavoursome Food

Stir-frying is one of the most versatile ways to cook many savoury foods. The wok is used to heat vegetables quickly, using a

small quantity of fat, yet preserving all the natural goodness and benefits of eating fresh vegetables. By adding a variety of different herbs and spices, sumptuous meat-free main courses are created in seconds. Moreover, rice and noodles, which are high in carbohydrates and release energy slowly, are abundant in many of the dishes, and play an important part in

maintaining a healthy diet. The lack of high-cholesterol and high-fat ingredients in traditional stir-fry dishes is also a bonus. Dairy products and red meat are rarely present or are served sparingly.

Different Types of Stir-Frying

The art of stir-frying is to cook the food very quickly, tossing the ingredients in a round-based, cast-iron wok over a high heat. However, there are two different methods of stir-frying, producing very distinctive results. *Liu* is wet frying with less vigorous stirring and more turning of the food. A cornflour (cornstarch) and stock mixture is added with sugar, vinegar and soy sauce at the end of cooking for a delicious coating sauce. *Pao*, or explosion, requires foods to be fried at the highest heat, and it is a very short, sharp method of cooking, usually lasting about a minute. Foods cooked in this way are generally marinated beforehand to maintain flavour and tenderness.

Balancing the Yin and Yang

In traditional Chinese stir-frying there is a desire to achieve balance and harmony in the foods served. Spicy

dishes are complimented with sweet-and-sour ones, dry-cooked plates are balanced with those bathed in sauce, meat is matched with vegetables. Dishes are chosen to complement each other in texture, flavour and colour and it is incorrect to serve more than one dish with the same main ingredient. The ancient Taoist philosophy of Yin and Yang, in which balance and contrast are the key, is what authentic cooks strive towards. In order for you to try this at home, a combination of dishes with different flavours and textures have been included.

Ingredients

Previously it was difficult for people in the West to cook traditional stir-fried food at home because many of the ingredients were hard to come by. Nowadays, with the presence of Chinese supermarkets and the familiarity of Asian foods in general, it is much easier to purchase items such as pak choi and good-quality black bean sauce. In order to add an authentic taste to your stir-fry dishes it is not only a good-quality wok that is

important but a selection of fine oils, excellent sauces and fresh vegetables. Some of the most important and unusual ingredients are listed below:

Chinese rice wine: Made from glutinous rice, this has a rich, sherry-like flavour and is golden in colour. The best is Shaoxing and is well matured and quite expensive. Avoid Mao Tai as this is a spirit stronger than vodka.

Dried mushrooms: Also known as shiitake mushrooms, these are used in many dishes. They are expensive, but as their flavour is strong, few are required. Soak them in hot water for 20–30 minutes before using.

Ginger: The fresh root is essential in many stir-fries. Ground ginger is no substitute as it will burn during cooking and does not give the same delicate flavour. Choose plump sections of root with shiny, unblemished skins.

Hoisin sauce: Sweet and spicy, this dark brownish-red sauce is often combined with soy sauce for flavouring stir-fries. It is sometimes provided in a small bowl at the table as a dipping sauce.

Oyster sauce: Made from boiled oysters and soy sauce, this salty, brown sauce should be used moderately. It is widely used in Cantonese cooking. Vegetarians can use soy sauce as a substitute.

Pak choi: A Member of the cabbage family, it has a mild, uncabbage-like flavour when cooked. It is excellent for stir-frying but can also be boiled.

Tofu: Also called bean curd. On its own it has a bland flavour, but it readily absorbs flavours from other ingredients. Firm tofu is best for stir-frying and is sold in cakes. It is high in protein, making it popular with vegetarians.

KEY

 Simplicity level 1 – 3 (1 easiest, 3 slightly harder)

 Preparation time

 Cooking time

Chicken & Noodle Salad

Strips of chicken are coated in a delicious spicy mixture, then stir-fried with noodles and served on a bed of salad.

NUTRITIONAL INFORMATION

Calories . . . . .217 Sugars 1g

Protein . . . . .21g Fat 11g

Carbohydrate . . . .9g Saturates 2g

🍲 🍲 🍲

🍲 10 MINS   ⏱ 10 MINS

SERVES 4

I N G R E D I E N T S

1 tsp finely grated fresh ginger root

½ tsp Chinese five-spice powder

1 tbsp plain (all-purpose) flour

½ tsp chilli powder

350 g/12 oz boned chicken breast, skinned and sliced thinly

60 g/2 oz rice noodles

125 g/4½ oz/1½ cups Chinese leaves (cabbage) or hard white cabbage, shredded finely

7 cm/3 inch piece of cucumber, sliced finely

1 large carrot, pared thinly

1 tbsp olive oil

2 tbsp lime or lemon juice

2 tbsp sesame oil

salt and pepper

TO GARNISH

lemon or lime slices

fresh coriander (cilantro) leaves

3 Mix together the Chinese leaves (cabbage) or white cabbage, cucumber and carrot, and arrange in a salad bowl. Whisk together the olive oil and lime or lemon juice, season with a salt and pepper, and use to dress the salad.

4 Heat the sesame oil in a wok or frying pan (skillet) and add the chicken. Stir-fry for 5–6 minutes until well-browned and crispy on the outside. Remove from the wok or frying pan (skillet) with a perforated spoon and drain on absorbent kitchen paper (paper towels).

5 Add the noodles to the wok or frying pan (skillet) and stir-fry for 3–4 minutes until heated through. Remove from the wok, mix with the chicken and pile the mixture on top of the salad. Serve garnished with lime or lemon slices and coriander (cilantro) leaves.

1 Mix together the ginger, five-spice powder, flour and chilli powder in a shallow mixing bowl. Season with salt and pepper. Add the strips of chicken and roll in the mixture until well coated.

2 Put the noodles into a large bowl and cover with warm water. Leave to soak for about 5 minutes, then drain them well.

Sweet & Sour Tofu Salad

Tofu (bean curd) is a delicious, healthy alternative to meat. Mixed with crisp stir-fried vegetables it makes an ideal light meal or starter.

NUTRITIONAL INFORMATION

Calories 262   Sugars 15g
Protein ....16g   Fat 14g
Carbohydrate ...19g   Saturates 2g

10 MINS   15 MINS

SERVES 4

I N G R E D I E N T S

2 tbsp vegetable oil

1 garlic clove, crushed

500 g/1 lb 2 oz tofu (bean curd), cubed

1 onion, sliced

1 carrot, cut into julienne strips

1 stick celery, sliced

2 small red (bell) peppers, cored, seeded and sliced

250 g/9 oz mangetout (snow peas), trimmed and halved

125 g/4½ oz broccoli, trimmed and divided into florets

125g/4½ oz thin green beans, halved

2 tbsp oyster sauce

1 tbsp tamarind concentrate

1 tbsp fish sauce

1 tbsp tomato purée (paste)

1 tbsp light soy sauce

1 tbsp chilli sauce

2 tbsp sugar

1 tbsp white vinegar

pinch of ground star anise

1 tsp cornflour (cornstarch)

300 ml/½ pint/1¼ cups water

1 Heat the vegetable oil in a large, heavy-based frying pan (skillet) or wok until hot.

2 Add the crushed garlic to the wok or pan and cook for a few seconds.

3 Add the tofu (bean curd), in batches, and stir-fry over a gentle heat, until golden on all sides. Remove with a slotted spoon and keep warm.

4 Add the onion, carrot, celery, red (bell) pepper, mangetout (snow peas), broccoli and green beans to the pan and stir-fry for about 2–3 minutes or until tender-crisp.

5 Add the oyster sauce, tamarind concentrate, fish sauce, tomato purée (paste), soy sauce, chilli sauce, sugar, vinegar and star anise, mixing well to blend. Stir-fry for a further 2 minutes.

6 Mix the cornflour (cornstarch) with the water and add to the pan with the fried tofu (bean curd). Stir-fry gently until the sauce boils and thickens slightly.

7 Transfer the sweet and sour tofu (bean curd) salad to warm serving plates and serve immediately.

Chinese Hot Salad

This salad can also be eaten cold – add 3–4 tablespoons French dressing as the vegetables cool, toss well and serve cold or chilled.

NUTRITIONAL INFORMATION

Calories 192   Sugars 13g
Protein ....5g   Fat 9g
Carbohydrate ...20g   Saturates 1g

5 MINS   10 MINS

SERVES 4

I N G R E D I E N T S

1 tbsp dark soy sauce

1½–2 tsp bottled sweet chilli sauce

2 tbsp sherry

1 tbsp brown sugar

1 tbsp wine vinegar

2 tbsp sunflower oil

1 garlic clove, crushed

4 spring onions (scallions), thinly sliced diagonally

250 g/9 oz courgettes (zucchini), cut into julienne strips about 4 cm/1½ inches long

250 g/9 oz carrots, cut into julienne strips about 4 cm/1½ inches long

1 red or green (bell) pepper, cored, seeded and thinly sliced

1 x 400 g/14 ½ oz can bean sprouts, well drained

125 g/4½ oz French (green) or fine beans, cut into 5 cm/2 inch lengths

1 tbsp sesame oil

salt and pepper

1–2 tsp sesame seeds, to garnish

1 Combine the soy sauce, chilli sauce, sherry, sugar, vinegar and seasoning.

2 Heat the 2 tablespoons of sunflower oil in a wok or large, heavy-based frying pan (skillet), swirling it around until it is really hot.

3 Add the garlic and spring onions (scallions) to the wok and stir-fry for 1–2 minutes.

4 Add the courgettes (zucchini), carrots and (bell) peppers and stir-fry for 1–2 minutes, then add the soy sauce mixture and bring to the boil.

5 Add the bean sprouts and French (green) beans and stir-fry for 1–2 minutes, making sure all the vegetables are thoroughly coated with the sauce.

6 Drizzle the sesame oil over the vegetables in the wok and stir-fry for about 30 seconds.

7 Serve the salad hot, sprinkled with sesame seeds.

Stir-Fried Chilli Cucumber

Warm cucumbers are absolutely delicious, especially when combined with the heat of chilli and the flavour of ginger.

NUTRITIONAL INFORMATION

Calories	67	Sugars	........4g
Protein	.........1g	Fat	..........5g
Carbohydrate	....5g	Saturates	.......1g

  30 MINS   5 MINS

SERVES 4

I N G R E D I E N T S

2 medium cucumbers

2 tsp salt

1 tbsp vegetable oil

2 garlic cloves, crushed

1-cm/½-inch fresh root ginger, grated

2 fresh red chillies, chopped

2 spring onions (scallions), chopped

1 tsp yellow bean sauce

1 tbsp clear honey

125 ml/4 fl oz/½ cup water

1 tsp sesame oil

1 Peel the cucumbers and cut in half lengthways. Scrape the seeds from the centre with a teaspoon or melon baller and discard.

2 Cut the cucumber into strips and place on a plate. Sprinkle the salt over the cucumber strips and set aside for 20 minutes. Rinse well under cold running water and pat dry with absorbent kitchen paper (paper towels).

3 Heat the vegetable oil in a preheated wok or large frying pan (skillet) until it is almost smoking. Lower the heat slightly and add the garlic, ginger, chillies and spring onions (scallions) and stir-fry for 30 seconds.

4 Add the cucumbers to the wok, together with the yellow bean sauce and honey and stir-fry for 30 seconds.

5 Add the water and cook over a high heat until most of the water has evaporated.

6 Sprinkle the sesame oil over the stir-fry. Transfer to a warm serving dish and serve immediately.

COOK'S TIP

The cucumber is sprinkled with salt and left to stand in order to draw out the excess water, thus preventing a soggy meal!

Orange Chicken Stir-Fry

Chicken thighs are inexpensive, meaty portions which are readily available. Although not as tender as breast, it is perfect for stir-frying.

NUTRITIONAL INFORMATION

Calories	267	Sugars	........11g
Protein	........23g	Fat	...........11g
Carbohydrate	...15g	Saturates	.......2g

 10 MINS   15 MINS

SERVES 4

INGREDIENTS

3 tbsp sunflower oil

350 g/12 oz boneless chicken thighs, skinned and cut into thin strips

1 onion, sliced

1 clove garlic, crushed

1 red (bell) pepper, deseeded and sliced

75 g/2¾ oz/1¼ cups mangetout (snow peas)

4 tbsp light soy sauce

4 tbsp sherry

1 tbsp tomato purée (tomato paste)

finely grated rind and juice of 1 orange

1 tsp cornflour (cornstarch)

2 oranges

100 g/3½ oz/1 cup bean sprouts

cooked rice or noodles, to serve

1 Heat the oil in a large preheated wok. Add the chicken and stir-fry for 2–3 minutes or until sealed on all sides.

2 Add the onion, garlic, (bell) pepper and mangetout (snow peas) to the wok. Stir-fry for a further 5 minutes, or until the vegetables are just tender and the chicken is completely cooked through.

3 Mix together the soy sauce, sherry, tomato purée (tomato paste), orange rind and juice and the cornflour (cornstarch). Add to the wok and cook, stirring, until the juices start to thicken.

4 Using a sharp knife, peel and segment the oranges. Add the segments to the mixture in the wok with the bean sprouts and heat through for a further 2 minutes.

5 Transfer the stir-fry to serving plates and serve at once with cooked rice or noodles.

COOK'S TIP

Bean sprouts are sprouting mung beans and are a regular ingredient in Chinese cooking. They require very little cooking and may even be eaten raw, if wished.

Oyster Sauce Lamb

This really is a speedy dish, lamb leg steaks being perfect for the short cooking time.

NUTRITIONAL INFORMATION

Calories ....243 Sugars 0.4g
Protein ....26g Fat 14g
Carbohydrate ....3g Saturates 5g

 5 MINS   10 MINS

SERVES 4

I N G R E D I E N T S

450 g/1 lb lamb leg steaks

1 tsp ground Szechuan peppercorns

1 tbsp groundnut oil

2 cloves garlic, crushed

8 spring onions (scallions), sliced

2 tbsp dark soy sauce

6 tbsp oyster sauce

175 g/6 oz Chinese leaves (cabbage)

prawn (shrimp) crackers, to serve
(optional)

1 Using a sharp knife, remove any excess fat from the lamb. Slice the lamb thinly.

2 Sprinkle the ground Szechuan peppercorns over the meat and toss together until well combined.

3 Heat the groundnut oil in a preheated wok or large heavy-based frying pan (skillet).

4 Add the lamb to the wok or frying pan (skillet) and stir-fry for about 5 minutes.

5 Meanwhile, crush the garlic cloves in a pestle and mortar and slice the spring onions (scallions). Add the garlic and spring onions (scallions) to the wok together with the dark soy sauce and stir-fry for 2 minutes.

6 Add the oyster sauce and Chinese leaves (cabbage) and stir-fry for a further 2 minutes, or until the leaves have wilted and the juices are bubbling.

7 Transfer the stir-fry to warm serving bowls and serve hot with prawn (shrimp) crackers (if using).

COOK'S TIP

Oyster sauce is made from oysters which are cooked in brine and soy sauce. Sold in bottles, it will keep in the refrigerator for months.

Red Spiced Beef

A spicy stir-fry flavoured with paprika, chilli and tomato, with a crisp bite to it from the celery strips.

NUTRITIONAL INFORMATION

Calories . . . . .431 Sugars 0g
Protein . . . . .32g Fat 28g
Carbohydrate . . .14g Saturates 10g

40 MINS   10 MINS

SERVES 4

INGREDIENTS

625 g/1 lb 6 oz sirloin or rump steak

2 tbsp paprika

2–3 tsp mild chilli powder

½ tsp salt

6 celery sticks

4 tomatoes, peeled, seeded and sliced

6 tbsp stock or water

2 tbsp tomato purée (paste)

2 tbsp clear honey

3 tbsp wine vinegar

1 tbsp Worcestershire sauce

2 tbsp sunflower oil

4 spring onions (scallions), thinly sliced diagonally

1–2 garlic cloves, crushed

Chinese noodles, to serve

celery leaves, to garnish (optional)

1 Using a sharp knife or meat cleaver, cut the steak across the grain into narrow strips 1 cm/½ inch thick and place in a bowl.

2 Combine the paprika, chilli powder and salt, add to the beef and mix thoroughly until the meat strips are evenly coated with the spices. Leave the beef to marinate in a cool place for at least 30 minutes.

3 Cut the celery into 5 cm/2 inch lengths, then cut the lengths into strips about 5 mm/¼ inch thick.

4 Combine the stock, tomato purée (paste), honey, wine vinegar and Worcestershire sauce and set aside.

5 Heat the oil in the wok until really hot. Add the spring onion (scallions), celery and garlic and stir-fry for about 1 minute until the vegetables are beginning to soften, then add the steak strips. Stir-fry over a high heat for 3–4 minutes until the meat is well sealed.

6 Add the sauce to the wok and continue to stir-fry briskly until thoroughly coated and sizzling.

7 Serve with noodles and garnish with celery leaves, if liked.

Lamb with Black Bean Sauce

Red onions add great colour to recipes and are perfect in this dish, combining with the colours of the (bell) peppers.

NUTRITIONAL INFORMATION

Calories 328   Sugars 5g
Protein . . . . .26g   Fat 20g
Carbohydrate . . .12g   Saturates 6g

 10 MINS   15 MINS

SERVES 4

INGREDIENTS

450 g/1 lb lamb neck fillet or boneless
   leg of lamb chops

1 egg white, lightly beaten

25 g/1 oz/4 tbsp cornflour (cornstarch)

1 tsp Chinese five spice powder

3 tbsp sunflower oil

1 red onion

1 red (bell) pepper, deseeded
   and sliced

1 green (bell) pepper, deseeded
   and sliced

1 yellow or orange (bell) pepper,
   deseeded and sliced

5 tbsp black bean sauce

boiled rice or noodles, to serve

1 Using a sharp knife, slice the lamb into very thin strips.

2 Mix together the egg white, cornflour (cornstarch) and Chinese five-spice powder. Toss the lamb strips in the mixture until evenly coated.

3 Heat the oil in a wok and stir-fry the lamb over a high heat for 5 minutes or until it crispens around the edges.

4 Slice the red onion. Add the onion and (bell) pepper slices to the wok and stir-fry for 5–6 minutes, or until the vegetables just begin to soften.

5 Stir the black bean sauce into the mixture in the wok and heat through.

6 Transfer the lamb and sauce to warm serving plates and serve hot with freshly boiled rice or noodles.

COOK'S TIP

Take care when frying the lamb as the cornflour (cornstarch) mixture may cause it to stick to the wok. Move the lamb around the wok constantly during stir-frying.

Beef with Green Peas

This recipe is the perfect example of quick stir-frying ingredients for a delicious, crisp, colourful dish.

NUTRITIONAL INFORMATION

Calories 325	Sugars 2g	
Protein 26g	Fat 22g	
Carbohydrate 8g	Saturates 7g	

5 MINS 10 MINS

SERVES 4

INGREDIENTS

450 g/1 lb rump steak

2 tbsp sunflower oil

1 onion

2 cloves garlic

150 g/5½oz/1 cup fresh or frozen peas

160 g/5¾oz jar black bean sauce

150 g/5½ oz Chinese leaves (cabbage), shredded

1 Using a sharp knife, trim away any fat from the beef. Cut the beef into thin slices.

2 Heat the sunflower oil in a large preheated wok.

3 Add the beef to the wok and stir-fry for 2 minutes.

4 Using a sharp knife, peel and slice the onion and crush the garlic cloves in a pestle and mortar.

5 Add the onion, garlic and peas to the wok and stir-fry for 5 minutes.

6 Add the black bean sauce and Chinese leaves (cabbage) to the wok.

7 Heat the mixture in the wok for a further 2 minutes until the Chinese leaves (cabbage) have wilted.

8 Transfer to warm serving bowls then serve immediately.

COOK'S TIP

Buy a chunky black bean sauce if you can for the best texture and flavour.

Chinese leaves (cabbage) are now widely available. They look like a pale, elongated head of lettuce with light green, tightly packed crinkly leaves.

Stir-Fried Pork & Cabbage

Rustle up this quick dish in a matter of moments. Assemble all your ingredients first, then everything is ready to hand as you start to stir-fry.

NUTRITIONAL INFORMATION

Calories 226	Sugars 2g
Protein 21g	Fat 12g
Carbohydrate 4g	Saturates 3g

5 MINS   10 MINS

SERVES 4

INGREDIENTS

375 g/13 oz pork fillet (tenderloin)

8 spring onions (scallions), trimmed

½ small white cabbage

½ cucumber

2 tsp finely grated fresh ginger root

1 tbsp fish sauce or light soy sauce

2 tbsp dry sherry

2 tbsp water

2 tsp cornflour (cornstarch)

1 tbsp chopped fresh mint or coriander (cilantro)

2 tbsp sesame oil

salt and pepper

TO GARNISH

sprigs of fresh mint or coriander (cilantro)

1 chilli flower (see Cook's Tip, right)

1 Slice the pork very thinly. Shred the spring onions (scallions) and cabbage, and cut the cucumber into matchsticks.

2 Mix together the ginger, fish sauce or soy sauce, sherry, water, cornflour (cornstarch) and chopped mint or coriander (cilantro) until blended.

3 Heat the sesame oil in a wok and add the pork. Stir-fry briskly over a high heat until browned, about 4–5 minutes.

4 Add the spring onions (scallions), cabbage and cucumber and stir-fry for a further 2 minutes. Add the cornflour (cornstarch) mixture and continue to cook for about 1 minute, until slightly thickened. Season to taste.

5 Transfer the stir-fry to a warmed dish and serve at once, garnished with sprigs of fresh mint or coriander (cilantro) and a chilli flower.

COOK'S TIP

To make chilli flowers, hold the stem of the chilli and cut down its length several times with a sharp knife. Place in a bowl of chilled water and chill so that the 'petals' turn out. Remove the chilli seeds when the 'petals' have opened.

Green Chicken Stir-Fry

Tender chicken is mixed with a selection of spring greens and flavoured with yellow bean sauce in this crunchy stir-fry.

NUTRITIONAL INFORMATION

Calories 297	Sugars 5g
Protein 30g	Fat 16g
Carbohydrate 8g	Saturates 3g

5 MINS   15 MINS

SERVES 4

INGREDIENTS

2 tbsp sunflower oil

450 g/1 lb skinless, boneless chicken breasts

2 cloves garlic, crushed

1 green (bell) pepper

100 g/3½ oz/1½ cups mangetout (snow peas)

6 spring onions (scallions), sliced, plus extra to garnish

225 g/8 oz spring greens or cabbage, shredded

160 g/5¾ oz jar yellow bean sauce

50 g/1¾ oz/3 tbsp roasted cashew nuts

1 Heat the sunflower oil in a large preheated wok.

2 Slice the chicken into thin strips and add to the wok together with the garlic. Stir-fry for about 5 minutes or until the chicken is sealed on all sides and beginning to turn golden.

3 Using a sharp knife, deseed the green (bell) pepper and cut into thin strips.

4 Add the mangetout (snow peas), spring onions (scallions), green (bell) pepper strips and spring greens or cabbage to the wok. Stir-fry for a further 5 minutes or until the vegetables are just tender.

5 Stir in the yellow bean sauce and heat through for about 2 minutes or until the mixture starts to bubble.

6 Scatter the roasted cashew nuts into the wok.

7 Transfer the stir-fry to warm serving plates and garnish with extra spring onions (scallions), if desired. Serve the stir-fry immediately.

COOK'S TIP

Do not add salted cashew nuts to this dish otherwise the dish will be too salty.

Stir-Fried Rice with Sausage

This is a very quick rice dish as it uses pre-cooked rice. It is therefore ideal when time is short or for a quick lunch-time dish.

NUTRITIONAL INFORMATION

Calories	383	Sugars	.........9g
Protein	........19g	Fat	..........17g
Carbohydrate	...42g	Saturates	.......4g

 5 MINS   20 MINS

SERVES 4

I N G R E D I E N T S

350 g/12 oz Chinese sausage

2 tbsp sunflower oil

2 tbsp soy sauce

1 onion, sliced

175 g/6 oz carrots, cut into thin sticks

175 g/6 oz/1¼ cups peas

100 g/3½ oz/¾ cup canned pineapple cubes, drained

275 g/9½ oz/4¾ cups cooked long-grain rice

1 egg, beaten

1 tbsp chopped fresh parsley

1 Using a sharp knife, thinly slice the Chinese sausage.

2 Heat the sunflower oil in a large preheated wok. Add the sausage to the wok and stir-fry for 5 minutes.

3 Stir in the soy sauce and allow to bubble for about 2–3 minutes, or until syrupy.

4 Add the onion, carrots, peas and pineapple to the wok and stir-fry for a further 3 minutes.

5 Add the cooked rice to the wok and stir-fry the mixture for about 2–3 minutes, or until the rice is completely heated through.

6 Drizzle the beaten egg over the top of the rice and cook, tossing the ingredients in the wok, until the egg sets.

7 Transfer the stir-fried rice to a large, warm serving bowl and scatter with plenty of chopped fresh parsley. Serve immediately.

COOK'S TIP

Cook extra rice and freeze it in prepration for other rice dishes as it saves time and enables a meal to be prepared in minutes. Be sure to cool any leftover cooked rice quickly before freezing to avoid food poisoning.

Chicken & Ginger Stir-Fry

The pomegranate seeds add a sharp Chinese flavour to this Indian stir-fry. Serve in the summer with a spicy rice salad or a mixed green salad.

NUTRITIONAL INFORMATION

Calories 291   Sugars 0g
Protein ....41g   Fat 14g
Carbohydrate ....0g   Saturates 3g

 10 MINS   25 MINS

SERVES 4

I N G R E D I E N T S

3 tbsp oil

700 g/1 lb 9 oz lean skinless, boneless chicken breasts, cut into 5 cm/2 inch strips

3 garlic cloves, crushed

3.5 cm/1½ inch piece fresh ginger root, cut into strips

1 tsp pomegranate seeds, crushed

½ tsp ground turmeric

1 tsp garam masala

2 fresh green chillies, sliced

½ tsp salt

4 tbsp lemon juice

grated rind of 1 lemon

6 tbsp chopped fresh coriander (cilantro)

125 ml/4 fl oz/½ cup chicken stock

naan bread, to serve

1 Heat the oil in a wok or large frying pan (skillet) and stir-fry the chicken until golden brown all over. Remove from the pan and set aside.

2 Add the garlic, ginger and pomegranate seeds to the pan and fry in the oil for 1 minute taking care not to let the garlic burn.

3 Stir in the turmeric, garam masala and chillies, and fry for 30 seconds.

4 Return the chicken to the pan and add the salt, lemon juice, lemon rind, coriander (cilantro) and stock. Stir the chicken well to make sure it is coated in the sauce.

5 Bring the mixture to the boil, then lower the heat and simmer for 10–15 minutes until the chicken is thoroughly cooked. Serve with warm naan bread.

COOK'S TIP

Stir-frying is perfect for low-fat diets as only a little oil is needed. Cooking the food over a high temperature ensures that food is sealed and cooked quickly to hold in the flavour.

Fruity Duck Stir-Fry

The pineapple and plum sauce add a sweetness and fruity flavour to this colourful recipe which blends well with the duck.

NUTRITIONAL INFORMATION

Calories 241	Sugars 7g	
Protein 26g	Fat 8g	
Carbohydrate ...16g	Saturates 2g	

 5 MINS   25 MINS

SERVES 4

INGREDIENTS

4 duck breasts

1 tsp Chinese five-spice powder

1 tbsp cornflour (cornstarch)

1 tbsp chilli oil

225 g/8 oz baby onions, peeled

2 cloves garlic, crushed

100 g/3½ oz/1 cup baby corn cobs

175 g/6 oz/1¼ cups canned pineapple chunks

6 spring onions (scallions), sliced

100 g/3½ oz/1 cup bean sprouts

2 tbsp plum sauce

1 Remove any skin from the duck breasts. Cut the duck into thin slices.

2 Mix the five-spice powder and the cornflour (cornstarch). Toss the duck in the mixture until well coated.

3 Heat the oil in a preheated wok. Stir-fry the duck for 10 minutes, or until just begining to crispen around the edges. Remove from the wok and set aside.

4 Add the onions and garlic to the wok and stir-fry for 5 minutes, or until softened. Add the baby corn cobs and stir-fry for a further 5 minutes. Add the pineapple, spring onions (scallions) and bean sprouts and stir-fry for 3–4 minutes. Stir in the plum sauce.

5 Return the cooked duck to the wok and toss until well mixed. Transfer to warm serving dishes and serve hot.

COOK'S TIP

Buy pineapple chunks in natural juice rather than syrup for a fresher flavour. If you can only obtain pineapple in syrup, rinse it in cold water and drain thoroughly before using.

Chicken with Vegetables

Coconut adds a creamy texture and delicious flavour to this stir-fry, which is spiked with green chilli.

NUTRITIONAL INFORMATION

Calories ......330 Sugars 4g
Protein ....23g Fat 24g
Carbohydrate ....6g Saturates 10g

10 MINS   10 MINS

SERVES 4

I N G R E D I E N T S

3 tbsp sesame oil

350 g/12 oz chicken breast, sliced thinly

8 shallots, sliced

2 garlic cloves, finely chopped

2.5 cm/1 inch piece fresh root ginger, grated

1 green chilli, finely chopped

1 each red and green (bell) pepper, sliced thinly

3 courgettes (zucchini), thinly sliced

2 tbsp ground almonds

1 tsp ground cinnamon

1 tbsp oyster sauce

50 g/1¾ oz/¼ cup creamed coconut, grated

salt and pepper

1 Heat the sesame oil in a preheated wok or large frying pan (skillet).

2 Add the chicken slices to the wok or frying pan (skillet), season with salt and pepper and stir-fry for about 4 minutes.

3 Add the shallots, garlic, ginger and chilli and stir-fry for 2 minutes.

4 Add the red and green (bell) peppers and courgettes (zucchini) and cook for about 1 minute.

5 Finally, add the ground almonds, cinnamon, oyster sauce and coconut. Stir-fry for 1 minute.

6 Transfer to a warm serving dish and serve immediately.

VARIATION

You can vary the vegetables in this dish according to seasonal availability or whatever you have at hand. Try broccoli florets or baby sweetcorn cobs.

Duck with Leek & Cabbage

Duck is a strongly-flavoured meat which benefits from the added citrus peel to counteract this rich taste.

NUTRITIONAL INFORMATION

Calories	192	Sugars	.........5g
Protein	........26g	Fat	...........7g
Carbohydrate	....6g	Saturates	.......2g

🔥🔥

10 MINS   🕐 40 MINS

SERVES 4

INGREDIENTS

4 duck breasts

350 g/12 oz green cabbage, thinly shredded

225 g/8 oz leeks, sliced

finely grated zest of 1 orange

6 tbsp oyster sauce

1 tsp toasted sesame seeds, to serve

1 Heat a large wok and dry-fry the duck breasts, with the skin on, for about 5 minutes on each side (you may need to do this in 2 batches).

2 Remove the duck breasts from the wok and transfer to a clean board.

3 Using a sharp knife, cut the duck breasts into thin slices.

4 Remove all but 1 tablespoon of the fat from the duck left in the wok; discard the rest.

5 Using a sharp knife, thinly shred the green cabbage.

6 Add the leeks, green cabbage and orange zest to the wok and stir-fry for about 5 minutes, or until the vegetables have softened.

7 Return the duck to the wok and heat through for 2–3 minutes.

8 Drizzle the oyster sauce over the mixture in the wok, toss well until all the ingredients are combined and then heat through.

9 Scatter the stir-fry with toasted sesame seeds, transfer to a warm serving dish and serve hot.

VARIATION

Use Chinese leaves (cabbage) for a lighter, sweeter flavour instead of the green cabbage, if you prefer.

Turkey with Cranberry Glaze

Traditional Christmas ingredients are given a Chinese twist in this stir-fry which contains cranberries, ginger, chestnuts and soy sauce!

NUTRITIONAL INFORMATION

Calories 167	Sugars 11g
Protein 8g	Fat 7g
Carbohydrate ...20g	Saturates 1g

5 MINS   15 MINS

SERVES 4

INGREDIENTS

1 turkey breast

2 tbsp sunflower oil

15 g/½oz/2 tbsp stem ginger

50 g/1¾ oz/½ cup fresh or frozen cranberries

100 g/3½ oz/¼ cup canned chestnuts

4 tbsp cranberry sauce

3 tbsp light soy sauce

salt and pepper

1 Remove any skin from the turkey breast. Using a sharp knife, thinly slice the turkey breast.

2 Heat the sunflower oil in a large preheated wok or heavy-based frying pan (skillet).

3 Add the turkey to the wok and stir-fry for 5 minutes, or until cooked through.

4 Using a sharp knife, finely chop the stem ginger.

5 Add the ginger and the cranberries to the wok or frying pan (skillet) and stir-fry for 2–3 minutes or until the cranberries have softened.

6 Add the chestnuts, cranberry sauce and soy sauce, season to taste with salt and pepper and allow to bubble for 2–3 minutes.

7 Transfer the turkey stir-fry to warm serving dishes and serve immediately.

COOK'S TIP

It is very important that the wok is very hot before you stir-fry. Test by by holding your hand flat about 7.5 cm/3 inches above the base of the interior – you should be able to feel the heat radiating from it.

Chicken & Corn Sauté

This quick and healthy dish is stir-fried, using only a minimum of fat.

NUTRITIONAL INFORMATION

Calories 280	Sugars 7g
Protein 31g	Fat 11g
Carbohydrate 9g	Saturates 2g

 5 MINS   10 MINS

SERVES 4

I N G R E D I E N T S

4 skinless, boneless chicken breasts

250 g/9 oz/1⅓ cups baby sweetcorn (corn-on-the-cob)

250 g/9 oz mangetout (snow peas)

2 tbsp sunflower oil

1 tbsp sherry vinegar

1 tbsp honey

1 tbsp light soy sauce

1 tbsp sunflower seeds

pepper

rice or Chinese egg noodles, to serve

1 Using a sharp knife, slice the chicken breasts into long, thin strips.

2 Cut the baby sweetcorn in half lengthways and top and tail the mangetout (snow peas).

3 Heat the sunflower oil in a preheated wok or a wide frying pan (skillet).

4 Add the chicken and fry over a fairly high heat, stirring, for 1 minute.

5 Add the baby sweetcorn and mangetout (snow peas) and stir-fry over a moderate heat for 5–8 minutes, until evenly cooked. The vegetables should still be slightly crunchy.

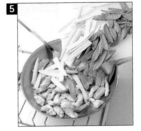

6 Mix together the sherry vinegar, honey and soy sauce in a small bowl.

7 Stir the vinegar mixture into the pan with the sunflower seeds.

8 Season well with pepper. Cook, stirring, for 1 minute.

9 Serve the chicken & corn sauté hot with rice or Chinese egg noodles.

VARIATION

Rice vinegar or balsamic vinegar makes a good substitute for the sherry vinegar.

Peanut Sesame Chicken

Sesame seeds and peanuts give extra crunch and flavour to this stir-fry and the fruit juice glaze gives a lovely shiny coating to the sauce.

 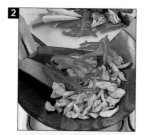 

NUTRITIONAL INFORMATION

Calories . . . . . . .435 Sugars 10g
Protein . . . . .38g Fat 26g
Carbohydrate . . .14g Saturates 4g

10 MINS   15 MINS

SERVES 4

INGREDIENTS

2 tbsp vegetable oil

2 tbsp sesame oil

500 g/1 lb 2 oz boneless, skinned chicken breasts, sliced into strips

250 g/9 oz broccoli, divided into small florets

250 g/9 oz baby or dwarf corn, halved if large

1 small red (bell) pepper, cored, seeded and sliced

2 tbsp soy sauce

250 ml/9 fl oz/1 cup orange juice

2 tsp cornflour (cornstarch)

2 tbsp toasted sesame seeds

60 g/2 oz/⅓ cup roasted, shelled, unsalted peanuts

rice or noodles, to serve

1 Heat the vegetable oil and sesame oil in a large, heavy-based frying pan (skillet) or wok until smoking. Add the chicken strips and stir-fry until browned, about 4–5 minutes.

2 Add the broccoli, corn and red (bell) pepper and stir-fry for a further 1–2 minutes.

3 Meanwhile, mix the soy sauce with the orange juice and cornflour (cornstarch). Stir into the chicken and vegetable mixture, stirring constantly until the sauce has slightly thickened and a glaze develops.

4 Stir in the sesame seeds and peanuts, mixing well. Heat the stir-fry for a further 3–4 minutes.

5 Transfer the stir-fry to a warm serving dish and serve with rice or noodles.

COOK'S TIP

Make sure you use the unsalted variety of peanuts or the dish will be too salty, as the soy sauce adds saltiness.

Sesame Lamb Stir-Fry

This is a very simple, but delicious dish, in which lean pieces of lamb are cooked in sugar and soy sauce and then sprinkled with sesame seeds.

NUTRITIONAL INFORMATION

Calories 276	Sugars 4g	
Protein 25g	Fat 18g	
Carbohydrate 5g	Saturates 6g	

 5 MINS   10 MINS

SERVES 4

I N G R E D I E N T S

450 g/1 lb boneless lean lamb

2 tbsp peanut oil

2 leeks, sliced

1 carrot, cut into matchsticks

2 garlic cloves, crushed

85 ml/3 fl oz/⅓ cup lamb or vegetable stock

2 tsp light brown sugar

1 tbsp dark soy sauce

4½ tsp sesame seeds

1 Using a sharp knife, cut the lamb into thin strips.

2 Heat the peanut oil in a preheated wok or large frying pan (skillet) until it is really hot.

3 Add the lamb and stir-fry for 2–3 minutes. Remove the lamb from the wok with a slotted spoon and set aside until required.

4 Add the leeks, carrot and garlic to the wok or frying pan (skillet) and stir-fry in the remaining oil for 1–2 minutes.

5 Remove the vegetables from the wok with a slotted spoon and set aside.

6 Drain any remaining oil from the wok. Place the lamb or vegetable stock,

light brown sugar and dark soy sauce in the wok and add the lamb. Cook, stirring constantly to coat the lamb, for 2–3 minutes.

7 Sprinkle the sesame seeds over the top, turning the lamb to coat.

8 Spoon the leek, carrot and garlic mixture on to a warm serving dish and top with the lamb. Serve immediately.

COOK'S TIP

Be careful not to burn the sugar in the wok when heating and coating the meat, otherwise the flavour of the dish will be spoiled.

Beef & Bok Choy

In this recipe, a colourful selection of vegetables is stir-fried with tender strips of steak.

NUTRITIONAL INFORMATION

Calories 369	Sugars 9g	
Protein 29g	Fat 23g	
Carbohydrate ...12g	Saturates 8g	

 15 MINS   5 MINS

SERVES 4

I N G R E D I E N T S

1 large head of bok choy, about
  250–275 g/9–9½ oz, torn into
  large pieces

2 tbsp vegetable oil

2 garlic cloves, crushed

500 g/1 lb 2 oz rump or fillet steak,
  cut into thin strips

150 g/5½ oz mangetout (snow peas),
  trimmed

150 g/5½ oz baby or dwarf corn

6 spring onions (scallions), chopped

2 red (bell) peppers, cored, seeded
  and thinly sliced

2 tbsp oyster sauce

1 tbsp fish sauce

1 tbsp sugar

rice or noodles, to serve

1 Steam the bok choy over boiling water until just tender. Keep warm.

2 Heat the oil in a large, heavy-based frying pan (skillet) or wok, add the garlic and steak strips and stir-fry until just browned, about 1–2 minutes.

3 Add the mangetout (snow peas), baby corn, spring onions (scallions), red (bell) pepper, oyster sauce, fish sauce and sugar to the pan, mixing well. Stir-fry for a further 2–3 minutes until the vegetables are just tender, but still crisp.

4 Arrange the bok choy leaves in the base of a heated serving dish and spoon the beef and vegetable mixture into the centre.

5 Serve the stir-fry immediately, with rice or noodles.

COOK'S TIP

Bok choy is one of the most important ingredients in this dish. If unavailable, use Chinese leaves (cabbage), kai choy (mustard leaves) or pak choi.

Stir-Fried Lamb with Orange

Oranges and lamb are a great combination because the citrus flavour offsets the fattier, fuller flavour of the lamb.

NUTRITIONAL INFORMATION

Calories 209	Sugars 4g
Protein 25g	Fat 10g
Carbohydrate 5g	Saturates 5g

 5 MINS 30 MINS

SERVES 4

I N G R E D I E N T S

450 g/1 lb minced (ground) lamb

2 cloves garlic, crushed

1 tsp cumin seeds

1 tsp ground coriander

1 red onion, sliced

finely grated zest and juice of
   1 orange

2 tbsp soy sauce

1 orange, peeled and segmented

salt and pepper

snipped fresh chives, to garnish

1 Heat a wok or large, heavy-based frying pan (skillet), without adding any oil.

2 Add the minced (ground) lamb to the wok. Dry fry the minced (ground) lamb for 5 minutes, or until the lamb is evenly browned. Drain away any excess fat from the wok.

3 Add the garlic, cumin seeds, ground coriander and red onion to the wok and stir-fry for a further 5 minutes.

4 Stir in the finely grated orange zest and juice and the soy sauce, mixing until thoroughly combined. Cover, reduce the heat and leave to simmer, stirring occasionally, for 15 minutes.

5 Remove the lid, increase the heat and add the orange segments. Stir to mix.

6 Season with salt and pepper to taste and heat through for a further 2–3 minutes.

7 Transfer the stir-fry to warm serving plates and garnish with snipped fresh chives. Serve immediately.

COOK'S TIP

If you wish to serve wine with your meal, try light, dry white wines and lighter Burgundy-style red wines as they blend well with Oriental food.

Stir-Fried Ginger Chicken

The oranges add colour and piquancy to this refreshing dish, which complements the chicken well.

NUTRITIONAL INFORMATION

Calories 289   Sugars 15g
Protein ....20g   Fat 9g
Carbohydrate ...17g   Saturates 2g

5 MINS   20 MINS

SERVES 4

INGREDIENTS

2 tbsp sunflower oil

1 onion, sliced

175 g/6 oz carrots, cut into thin sticks

1 clove garlic, crushed

350 g/12 oz boneless skinless chicken breasts

2 tbsp fresh ginger, peeled and grated

1 tsp ground ginger

4 tbsp sweet sherry

1 tbsp tomato purée (tomato paste)

1 tbsp demerara sugar

100 ml/3½ fl oz/⅓ cup orange juice

1 tsp cornflour (cornstarch)

1 orange, peeled and segmented

fresh snipped chives, to garnish

1 Heat the oil in a large preheated wok. Add the onion, carrots and garlic and stir-fry over a high heat for 3 minutes or until the vegetables begin to soften.

2 Slice the chicken into thin strips. Add to the wok with the fresh and ground ginger. Stir-fry for a further 10 minutes, or until the chicken is well cooked through and golden in colour.

3 Mix together the sherry, tomato purée (tomato paste), sugar, orange juice and cornflour (cornstarch) in a bowl. Stir the mixture into the wok and heat through until the mixture bubbles and the juices start to thicken.

4 Add the orange segments and carefully toss to mix.

5 Transfer the stir-fried chicken to warm serving bowls and garnish with freshly snipped chives. Serve immediately.

COOK'S TIP

Make sure that you do not continue cooking the dish once the orange segments have been added in step 4, otherwise they will break up.

Kung Po Chicken

In this recipe, cashew nuts are used but peanuts, walnuts or almonds can be substituted, if preferred.

NUTRITIONAL INFORMATION

Calories	294	Sugars	........3g
Protein	........21g	Fat	..........18g
Carbohydrate	...10g	Saturates	.......4g

10 MINS   5 MINS

SERVES 4

INGREDIENTS

250–300 g/9–10½ oz chicken meat, boned and skinned

¼ tsp salt

⅓ egg white

1 tsp cornflour (cornstarch) paste

1 medium green (bell) pepper, cored and seeded

4 tbsp vegetable oil

1 spring onion (scallion), cut into short sections

a few small slices of ginger root

4–5 small dried red chillies, soaked, seeded and shredded

2 tbsp crushed yellow bean sauce

1 tsp rice wine or dry sherry

125 g/4½ oz roasted cashew nuts

a few drops of sesame oil

boiled rice, to serve

1 Cut the chicken into small cubes about the size of sugar lumps. Place the chicken in a small bowl and mix with a pinch of salt, the egg white and the cornflour (cornstarch) paste, in that order.

2 Cut the green (bell) pepper into cubes or triangles about the same size as the chicken pieces.

3 Heat the oil in a wok, add the chicken and stir-fry for 1 minute. Remove with a slotted spoon and keep warm.

4 Add the spring onion (scallion), ginger, chillies and green (bell) pepper. Stir-fry for 1 minute, then add the chicken with the yellow bean sauce and wine. Blend well and stir-fry for another minute. Finally stir in the cashew nuts and sesame oil. Serve hot with boiled rice.

VARIATION

Any nuts can be used in place of the cashew nuts, if preferred. The important point is the crunchy texture, which is very much a feature of Szechuan cooking.

Chicken with Black Bean Sauce

This tasty chicken stir-fry is quick and easy to make and is full of fresh flavours and crunchy vegetables.

NUTRITIONAL INFORMATION

Calories . . . . . . .205 Sugars 4g
Protein . . . . .25g Fat 9g
Carbohydrate . . . .6g Saturates 2g

 40 MINS   10 MINS

SERVES 4

I N G R E D I E N T S

425 g/15 oz chicken breasts,
  sliced thinly

pinch of salt

pinch of cornflour (cornstarch)

2 tbsp oil

1 garlic clove, crushed

1 tbsp black bean sauce

1 each small red and green (bell) pepper,
  cut into strips

1 red chilli, chopped finely

75 g/2¾ oz/1 cup mushrooms, sliced

1 onion, chopped

6 spring onions (scallions), chopped

salt and pepper

S E A S O N I N G

½ tsp salt

½ tsp sugar

3 tbsp chicken stock

1 tbsp dark soy sauce

2 tbsp beef stock

2 tbsp rice wine

1 tsp cornflour (cornstarch), blended
  with a little rice wine

1 Put the chicken strips in a bowl. Add a pinch of salt and a pinch of cornflour (cornstarch) and cover with water. Leave to stand for 30 minutes.

2 Heat 1 tablespoon of the oil in a wok or deep-sided frying pan (skillet) and stir-fry the chicken for 4 minutes.

3 Remove the chicken to a warm serving dish and clean the wok.

4 Add the remaining oil to the wok and add the garlic, black bean sauce, green and red (bell) peppers, chilli, mushrooms, onion and spring onions (scallions). Stir-fry for 2 minutes then return the chicken to the wok.

5 Add the seasoning ingredients, fry for 3 minutes and thicken with a little of the cornflour (cornstarch) blend. Serve with fresh noodles.

Chilli Chicken

This is quite a hot dish, using fresh chillies. If you prefer a milder dish, halve the number of chillies used.

NUTRITIONAL INFORMATION

Calories 265   Sugars 3g
Protein . . . . .21g   Fat 14g
Carbohydrate . . . .11g   Saturates 2g

10 MINS   10 MINS

SERVES 4

I N G R E D I E N T S

350 g/12 oz skinless, boneless lean chicken

½ tsp salt

1 egg white, lightly beaten

2 tbsp cornflour (cornstarch)

4 tbsp vegetable oil

2 garlic cloves, crushed

1-cm/½-inch piece fresh root ginger, grated

1 red (bell) pepper, seeded and diced

1 green (bell) pepper, seeded and diced

2 fresh red chillies, chopped

2 tbsp light soy sauce

1 tbsp dry sherry or Chinese rice wine

1 tbsp wine vinegar

1 Cut the chicken into cubes and place in a mixing bowl.

2 Mix together the salt, egg white, cornflour (cornstarch) and 1 tablespoon of the oil and pour over the chicken. Turn the chicken in the mixture to coat thoroughly.

3 Heat the remaining oil in a preheated wok or large frying pan (skillet).

4 Add the garlic and ginger and stir-fry for 30 seconds.

5 Add the chicken pieces to the wok and stir-fry for 2–3 minutes, or until browned.

6 Stir in the red and green (bell) peppers, chillies, soy sauce, sherry or Chinese rice wine and wine vinegar and cook for a further 2–3 minutes, until the chicken is cooked through. Transfer the chilli chicken to a warm serving dish and serve immediately.

COOK'S TIP

When preparing chillies, wear rubber gloves to prevent the juices from burning and irritating your hands. Be careful not to touch your face, especially your lips or eyes, until you have washed your hands.

Stir-Fried Beef & Vegetables

Fillet of beef is perfect for stir-frying as it is so tender and lends itself to quick cooking.

NUTRITIONAL INFORMATION

Calories 521   Sugars 7g
Protein . . . . .31g   Fat 35g
Carbohydrate . . .18g   Saturates 8g

10 MINS   20 MINS

SERVES 4

INGREDIENTS

2 tbsp sunflower oil

350 g/12 oz fillet of beef, sliced

1 red onion, sliced

175 g/6 oz courgettes (zucchini)

175 g/6 oz carrots, thinly sliced

1 red (bell) pepper, deseeded and sliced

1 small head Chinese leaves (cabbage), shredded

150 g/5½ oz/1½ cups bean sprouts

225 g/8 oz can bamboo shoots, drained

150 g/5½ oz/½ cup cashew nuts, toasted

SAUCE

3 tbsp medium sherry

3 tbsp light soy sauce

1 tsp ground ginger

1 clove garlic, crushed

1 tsp cornflour (cornstarch)

1 tbsp tomato purée (paste)

1 Heat the sunflower oil in a large preheated wok. Add the sliced beef and red onion to the wok and stir-fry for about 4–5 minutes or until the onion begins to soften and the meat is just browning.

2 Trim the courgettes (zucchini) and slice diagonally.

3 Add the carrots, (bell) pepper, and courgettes (zucchini) to the wok and stir-fry for 5 minutes.

4 Toss in the Chinese leaves (cabbage), bean sprouts and bamboo shoots and heat through for 2–3 minutes, or until the leaves are just beginning to wilt.

5 Scatter the cashews nuts over the stir-fry and toss well to mix.

6 To make the sauce, mix together the sherry, soy sauce, ground ginger, garlic, cornflour (cornstarch) and tomato purée (tomato paste) until well combined.

7 Pour the sauce over the stir-fry and toss to mix. Allow the sauce to bubble for 2–3 minutes or until the juices thicken.

8 Transfer to warm serving dishes and serve at once.

Lamb & Ginger Stir-Fry

Slices of lamb cooked with garlic, ginger and shiitake mushrooms make a quick and easy supper. It is best served with Chinese egg noodles.

NUTRITIONAL INFORMATION

Calories	347	Sugars	........2g
Protein	........31g	Fat	..........21g
Carbohydrate	....7g	Saturates	.......7g

10 MINS   5 MINS

SERVES 4

I N G R E D I E N T S

500 g/1 lb 2 oz lamb fillet (tenderloin)

2 tbsp sunflower oil

1 tbsp chopped ginger root

2 garlic cloves, chopped

6 spring onions (scallions), white and
    green parts diagonally sliced

175 g/6 oz shiitake mushrooms, sliced

175 g/6 oz sugar snap peas

1 tsp cornflour (cornstarch)

2 tbsp dry sherry

1 tbsp light soy sauce

1 tsp sesame oil

1 tbsp sesame seeds, toasted

Chinese egg noodles, to serve

1 Using a sharp knife or meat cleaver, cut the lamb into 5 mm/^{1}/$_2$ inch slices.

2 Heat the sunflower oil in a large preheated wok or frying pan (skillet).

3 Add the lamb to the wok or frying pan (skillet) and stir-fry for 2 minutes.

4 Add the chopped ginger root, chopped garlic cloves, sliced spring onions (scallions), mushrooms and sugar snap peas and stir-fry for 2 minutes.

5 Blend the cornflour (cornstarch) with the sherry and stir into the wok.

6 Add the light soy sauce and sesame oil and cook, stirring, for 1 minute until thickened.

7 Sprinkle over the sesame seeds, transfer the lamb and ginger stir-fry to a warm serving dish and serve the stir-fry with Chinese egg noodles.

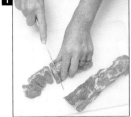

COOK'S TIP

Shiitake mushrooms are much used in Chinese cooking. They have a slightly meaty flavour and can be bought both fresh and dried. Their powerful flavour will permeate more bland mushrooms. Cook them briefly or they begin to toughen.

Pork Satay Stir-Fry

Satay sauce is easy to make and is one of the best known and loved sauces in Oriental cooking. It is perfect with beef, chicken or pork.

NUTRITIONAL INFORMATION

Calories . . . . . . .506 Sugars 11g
Protein . . . . .31g Fat 36g
Carbohydrate . . .15g Saturates 8g

 10 MINS   15 MINS

SERVES 4

INGREDIENTS

150 g/5½ oz carrots

2 tbsp sunflower oil

350 g/12 oz pork neck fillet, thinly sliced

1 onion, sliced

2 cloves garlic, crushed

1 yellow (bell) pepper, deseeded and sliced

150 g/5½ oz/2⅓ cups mangetout (snow peas)

75 g/2¾ oz/1½ cups fine asparagus

chopped salted peanuts, to serve

SATAY SAUCE

6 tbsp crunchy peanut butter

6 tbsp coconut milk

1 tsp chilli flakes

1 clove garlic, crushed

1 tsp tomato purée (paste)

COOK'S TIP

Cook the sauce just before serving as it tends to thicken very quickly and will not be spoonable if you cook it too far in advance.

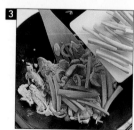

1 Using a sharp knife, slice the carrots into thin sticks.

2 Heat the oil in a large, preheated wok. Add the pork, onion and garlic and stir-fry for 5 minutes or until the lamb is cooked through.

3 Add the carrots, (bell) pepper, mangetout (snow peas) and asparagus to the wok and stir-fry for 5 minutes.

4 To make the satay sauce, place the peanut butter, coconut milk, chilli flakes, garlic and tomato purée (paste) in a small pan and heat gently, stirring, until well combined. Be careful not to let the sauce stick to the bottom of the pan.

5 Transfer the stir-fry to warm serving plates. Spoon the satay sauce over the stir-fry and scatter with chopped peanuts. Serve immediately.

Peppered Beef Cashew

A simple but stunning dish of tender strips of beef mixed with crunchy cashew nuts, coated in a hot sauce. Serve with rice noodles.

NUTRITIONAL INFORMATION

Calories 403   Sugars 7g
Protein . . . . .26g   Fat 29g
Carbohydrate . . . .11g   Saturates 9g

10 MINS   10 MINS

SERVES 4

INGREDIENTS

1 tbsp groundnut or sunflower oil

1 tbsp sesame oil

1 onion, sliced

1 garlic clove, crushed

1 tbsp grated ginger root

500 g/1 lb 2 oz fillet or rump steak, cut into thin strips

2 tsp palm sugar

2 tbsp light soy sauce

1 small yellow (bell) pepper, cored, seeded and sliced

1 red (bell) pepper, cored, seeded and sliced

4 spring onions (scallions), chopped

2 celery sticks, chopped

4 large open-cap mushrooms, sliced

4 tbsp roasted cashew nuts

3 tbsp stock or white wine

1 Heat the oils in a large, heavy-based frying pan (skillet) or wok. Add the onion, garlic and ginger and stir-fry for about 2 minutes until softened.

2 Add the steak strips and stir-fry for a further 2–3 minutes, until the meat has browned.

3 Add the sugar and soy sauce, stirring to mix well.

4 Add the (bell) peppers, spring onions (scallions), celery, mushrooms and cashews, mixing well.

5 Add the stock or white wine and stir-fry for 2–3 minutes until the beef is cooked through and the vegetables are tender-crisp.

6 Serve the stir-fry immediately with rice noodles.

COOK'S TIP

Palm sugar is a thick brown sugar with a slightly caramel taste. It is sold in cakes, or in small containers. If not available, use soft dark brown or demerara (brown crystal) sugar.

Gingered Monkfish

This dish is a real treat and is perfect for special occasions. Monkfish has a tender flavour which is ideal with asparagus, chilli and ginger.

NUTRITIONAL INFORMATION

Calories 133   Sugars 0g
Protein . . . . .21g   Fat 5g
Carbohydrate . . . .1g   Saturates 1g

5 MINS   10 MINS

SERVES 4

INGREDIENTS

450 g/1 lb monkfish

1 tbsp freshly grated root ginger

2 tbsp sweet chilli sauce

1 tbsp corn oil

100 g/3½ oz/1 cup fine asparagus

3 spring onions (scallions), sliced

1 tsp sesame oil

1 Using a sharp knife, slice the monkfish into thin flat rounds. Set aside until required.

2 Mix together the freshly grated root ginger and the sweet chilli sauce in a small bowl until thoroughly blended. Brush the ginger and chilli sauce mixture over the monkfish pieces, using a pastry brush.

COOK'S TIP

Monkfish is quite expensive, but it is well worth using as it has a wonderful flavour and texture. At a push you could use cubes of chunky cod fillet instead.

3 Heat the corn oil in a large preheated wok or heavy-based frying pan (skillet).

4 Add the monkfish pieces, asparagus and chopped spring onions (scallions) to the wok or frying pan (skillet) and cook for about 5 minutes, stirring gently so the fish pieces do not break up.

5 Remove the wok or frying pan (skillet) from the heat, drizzle the sesame oil over the stir-fry and toss well to combine.

6 Transfer the stir-fried gingered monkfish to warm serving plates and serve immediately.

Fried Prawns with Cashews

Cashew nuts are delicious as part of a stir-fry with almost any other ingredient. Use the unsalted variety in cooking.

NUTRITIONAL INFORMATION

Calories 406   Sugar 3g
Protein ....31g   Fat 25g
Carbohydrate ...13g   Saturates 4g

5 MINS   5 MINS

SERVES 4

INGREDIENTS

2 garlic cloves, crushed

1 tbsp cornflour (cornstarch)

pinch of caster (superfine) sugar

450 g/1 lb raw tiger prawns
   (jumbo shrimp)

4 tbsp vegetable oil

1 leek, sliced

125 g/4½ oz broccoli florets

1 orange (bell) pepper, seeded
   and diced

75 g/2¾oz/¾ cup unsalted
   cashew nuts

SAUCE

175 ml/6 fl oz/¾ cup fish stock

1 tbsp cornflour (cornstarch)

dash of chilli sauce

2 tsp sesame oil

1 tbsp Chinese rice wine

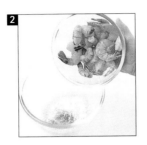
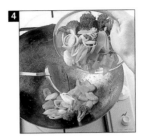

1 Mix together the garlic, cornflour (cornstarch) and sugar in a bowl.

2 Peel and devein the prawns (shrimp). Stir the prawns (shrimp) into the mixture to coat thoroughly.

3 Heat the vegetable oil in a preheated wok and add the prawn (shrimp) mixture. Stir-fry over a high heat for 20–30 seconds until the prawns (shrimp) turn pink. Remove the prawns (shrimp) from the wok with a slotted spoon, drain on absorbent kitchen paper (paper towels) and set aside until required.

4 Add the leek, broccoli and (bell) pepper to the wok and stir-fry for 2 minutes.

5 To make the sauce, place the fish stock, cornflour (cornstarch), chilli sauce to taste, the sesame oil and Chinese rice wine in a small bowl. Mix until thoroughly.

6 Add the sauce to the wok, together with the cashew nuts. Return the prawns (shrimp) to the wok and cook for 1 minute to heat through.

7 Transfer the prawn (shrimp) stir-fry to a warm serving dish and serve immediately.

Mussels in Black Bean Sauce

This dish looks so impressive, the combination of colours making it look almost too good to eat!

NUTRITIONAL INFORMATION

Calories	174	Sugars	.........4g
Protein	........19g	Fat	...........8g
Carbohydrate	....6g	Saturates	.......1g

5 MINS   10 MINS

SERVES 4

INGREDIENTS

350 g/12 oz leeks

350 g/12 oz cooked green-lipped mussels (shelled)

1 tsp cumin seeds

2 tbsp vegetable oil

2 cloves garlic, crushed

1 red (bell) pepper, deseeded and sliced

50 g/1¾ oz/¾ cup canned bamboo shoots, drained

175 g/6 oz baby spinach

160 g/5¾ oz jar black bean sauce

1 Using a sharp knife, trim the leeks and shred them.

2 Place the cooked green-lipped mussels in a large bowl, sprinkle with the cumin seeds and toss well to coat all over. Set aside until required.

COOK'S TIP

If the green-lipped mussels are not available they can be bought shelled in cans and jars from most large supermarkets.

3 Heat the vegetable oil in a preheated wok, swirling the oil around the base of the wok until it is really hot.

4 Add the shredded leeks, garlic and sliced red (bell) pepper to the wok and stir-fry for 5 minutes, or until the vegetables are tender.

5 Add the bamboo shoots, baby spinach leaves and cooked green-lipped mussels to the wok and stir-fry for about 2 minutes.

6 Pour the black bean sauce over the ingredients in the wok, toss well to coat all the ingredients in the sauce and leave to simmer for a few seconds, stirring occasionally.

7 Transfer the stir-fry to warm serving bowls and serve immediately.

Seafood Stir-Fry

This combination of assorted seafood and tender vegetables flavoured with ginger makes an ideal light meal served with thread noodles.

NUTRITIONAL INFORMATION

Calories ....226 Sugars 5g
Protein ....35g Fat 7g
Carbohydrate ....6g Saturates 1g

5 MINS   15 MINS

SERVES 4

INGREDIENTS

100 g/3½ oz small, thin asparagus spears, trimmed

1 tbsp sunflower oil

2.5 cm/1 inch piece root (fresh) ginger, cut into thin strips

1 medium leek, shredded

2 medium carrots, julienned

100 g/3½ oz baby sweetcorn cobs, quartered lengthwise

2 tbsp light soy sauce

1 tbsp oyster sauce

1 tsp clear honey

450 g/1 lb cooked, assorted shellfish, thawed if frozen

freshly cooked egg noodles, to serve

TO GARNISH

4 large cooked prawns

small bunch fresh chives, freshly snipped

1 Bring a small saucepan of water to the boil and blanch the asparagus for 1–2 minutes.

2 Drain the asparagus, set aside and keep warm.

3 Heat the oil in a wok or large frying pan (skillet) and stir-fry the ginger, leek, carrot and sweetcorn for about 3 minutes. Do not allow the vegetables to brown.

4 Add the soy sauce, oyster sauce and honey to the wok or frying pan (skillet).

5 Stir in the cooked shellfish and continue to stir-fry for 2–3 minutes until the vegetables are just tender and the shellfish are thoroughly heated through. Add the blanched asparagus and stir-fry for about 2 minutes.

6 To serve, pile the cooked noodles on to 4 warm serving plates and spoon the seafood and vegetable stir-fry over them.

7 Garnish with the cooked prawns and freshly snipped chives and serve immediately.

Stir-Fried Salmon with Leeks

Salmon is marinated in a deliciously rich, sweet sauce, stir-fried and served on a bed of crispy leeks.

NUTRITIONAL INFORMATION

Calories	360	Sugars	.........9g
Protein	........24g	Fat	..........25g
Carbohydrate	....11g	Saturates	.......4g

 35 MINS   15 MINS

SERVES 4

I N G R E D I E N T S

450 g/1 lb salmon fillet, skinned

2 tbsp sweet soy sauce

2 tbsp tomato ketchup (catsup)

1 tsp rice wine vinegar

1 tbsp demerara (brown crystal) sugar

1 clove garlic, crushed

4 tbsp corn oil

450 g/1 lb leeks, thinly shredded

finely chopped red chillies, to garnish

1 Using a sharp knife, cut the salmon into slices. Place the slices of salmon in a shallow non-metallic dish.

2 Mix together the soy sauce, tomato ketchup (catsup), rice wine vinegar, sugar and garlic.

3 Pour the mixture over the salmon, toss well and leave to marinate for about 30 minutes.

4 Meanwhile, heat 3 tablespoons of the corn oil in a large preheated wok.

5 Add the leeks to the wok and stir-fry over a medium-high heat for about 10 minutes, or until the leeks become crispy and tender.

6 Using a slotted spoon, carefully remove the leeks from the wok and transfer to warmed serving plates.

7 Add the remaining oil to the wok. Add the salmon and the marinade to the wok and cook for 2 minutes.

8 Remove the salmon from the wok and spoon over the leeks, garnish with finely chopped red chillies and serve immediately.

VARIATION

You can use a fillet of beef instead of the salmon, if you prefer.

Stir-Fried Prawns (Shrimp)

The (bell) peppers in this dish can be replaced by either mangetout (snow peas), or broccoli to maintain the attractive pink-green contrast.

NUTRITIONAL INFORMATION

Calories	116	Sugars	.........1g
Protein	........10g	Fat	...........6g
Carbohydrate	....4g	Saturates	.......1g

 5 MINS   10 MINS

SERVES 4

I N G R E D I E N T S

170 g/6 oz raw prawns (shrimp), peeled

1 tsp salt

¼ tsp egg white

2 tsp cornflour (cornstarch) paste

300 ml/½ pint/1¼ cups vegetable oil

1 spring onion (scallion), cut into short sections

2.5-cm/1-inch piece ginger root, thinly sliced

1 small green (bell) pepper, cored, seeded and cubed

½ tsp sugar

1 tbsp light soy sauce

1 tsp rice wine or dry sherry

a few drops sesame oil

VARIATION

1–2 small green or red hot chillies, sliced, can be added with the green (bell) pepper to create a more spicy dish. Leave the chillies unseeded for a very hot dish.

1 Mix the prawns (shrimp) with a pinch of the salt, the egg white and cornflour (cornstarch) paste until well coated.

2 Heat the oil in a preheated wok and stir-fry the prawns (shrimp) for 30–40 seconds only. Remove and drain on kitchen paper (paper towels).

3 Pour off the oil, leaving about 1 tablespoon in the wok. Add the spring onion (scallion) and ginger to flavour the oil for a few seconds, then add the green (bell) pepper and stir-fry for about 1 minute.

4 Add the remaining salt and the sugar followed by the prawns (shrimp). Continue stirring for another minute or so, then add the soy sauce and wine and blend well. Sprinkle with sesame oil and serve immediately.

Tuna & Vegetable Stir-Fry

Fresh tuna is a dark, meaty fish and is now widely available at fresh fish counters. It lends itself perfectly to the rich flavours in this recipe.

NUTRITIONAL INFORMATION

Calories	245	Sugars 11g
Protein	........30g	Fat 7g
Carbohydrate	...14g	Saturates 1g

10 MINS 10 MINS

SERVES 4

INGREDIENTS

225 g/8 oz carrots

1 onion

175 g/6 oz/1¾ cups baby corn cobs

2 tbsp corn oil

175 g/6 oz/2½ cups mangetout (snow peas)

450 g/1 lb fresh tuna

2 tbsp fish sauce

15 g/½ oz/1 tbsp palm sugar

finely grated zest and juice of 1 orange

2 tbsp sherry

1 tsp cornflour (cornstarch)

rice or noodles, to serve

1 Using a sharp knife, cut the carrots into thin sticks, slice the onion and halve the baby corn cobs.

2 Heat the corn oil in a large preheated wok or frying pan (skillet).

3 Add the onion, carrots, mangetout (snow peas) and baby corn cobs to the wok or frying pan (skillet) and stir-fry for 5 minutes.

4 Using a sharp knife, thinly slice the fresh tuna.

5 Add the tuna slices to the wok or frying pan (skillet) and stir-fry for

about 2–3 minutes, or until the tuna turns opaque.

6 Mix together the fish sauce, palm sugar, orange zest and juice, sherry and cornflour (cornstarch).

7 Pour the mixture over the tuna and vegetables and cook for 2 minutes, or until the juices thicken. Serve the stir-fry with rice or noodles.

VARIATION

Try using swordfish steaks instead of the tuna. Swordfish steaks are now widely available and are similar in texture to tuna

Squid with Black Bean Sauce

Squid really is wonderful if quickly cooked as in this recipe, and contrary to popular belief it is not tough and rubbery unless it is overcooked.

NUTRITIONAL INFORMATION

Calories 180   Sugars 2g
Protein ....19g   Fat 7g
Carbohydrate ...10g   Saturates 1g

 5 MINS   20 MINS

SERVES 4

INGREDIENTS

450 g/1 lb squid rings

2 tbsp plain (all-purpose) flour

½ tsp salt

1 green (bell) pepper

2 tbsp groundnut oil

1 red onion, sliced

160 g/5¾ oz jar black bean sauce

1 Rinse the squid rings under cold running water and pat dry thoroughly with absorbent kitchen paper (paper towels).

2 Place the plain (all-purpose) flour and salt in a bowl and mix together. Add the squid rings and toss until they are evenly coated.

3 Using a sharp knife, deseed the (bell) pepper. Slice the (bell) pepper into thin strips.

4 Heat the groundnut oil in a large preheated wok or heavy-based frying pan (skillet), swirling the oil around the base of the wok until it is really hot.

5 Add the (bell) pepper slices and red onion to the wok or frying pan (skillet) and stir-fry for about 2 minutes, or until the vegetables are just beginning to soften.

6 Add the squid rings to the wok or frying pan (skillet) and cook for a further 5 minutes, or until the squid is cooked through. Be careful not to overcook the squid.

7 Add the black bean sauce to the wok and heat through until the juices are bubbling. Transfer the squid stir-fry to warm serving bowls and serve immediately.

COOK'S TIP

Serve this recipe with fried rice or noodles tossed in soy sauce, if you wish.

Fish & Ginger Stir-Fry

This delicious and spicy recipe is a really quick fish dish, ideal for midweek family meals or light lunches at weekends.

NUTRITIONAL INFORMATION

Calories	280	Sugars	........2g
Protein	........31g	Fat	..........10g
Carbohydrate	...17g	Saturates	.......2g

 5 MINS   15 MINS

SERVES 4

I N G R E D I E N T S

4 tbsp cornflour (cornstarch)

½ tsp ground ginger

675 g/1½ lb firm white fish fillets, skinned and cubed

3 tbsp peanut oil

2.5-cm/1-inch fresh ginger root, grated

1 leek, thinly sliced

1 tbsp white wine vinegar

2 tbsp Chinese rice wine or dry sherry

3 tbsp dark soy sauce

1 tsp caster (superfine) sugar

2 tbsp lemon juice

finely shredded leek, to garnish

1 Mix the cornflour (cornstarch) and ground ginger in a bowl.

2 Add the cubes of fish, in batches, to the cornflour (cornstarch) mixture, turning to coat the fish thoroughly in the mixture.

3 Heat the peanut oil in a preheated wok or large, heavy-based frying pan (skillet), swirling the oil around the base of the wok until it is really hot.

4 Add the grated fresh ginger and sliced leek to the wok or frying pan (skillet) and stir-fry for 1 minute.

  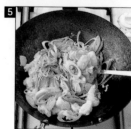

5 Add the coated fish to the wok and cook for a further 5 minutes, until browned, stirring to prevent the fish from sticking to the base of the wok.

6 Add the remaining ingredients and cook over a low heat for 3–4 minutes, until the fish is cooked through.

7 Transfer the fish and ginger stir-fry to a serving dish and serve immediately.

VARIATION

Use any firm white fish which will hold its shape, such as cod, haddock or monkfish.

Stir-Fried Cod with Mango

Fish and fruit are a classic combination, and in this recipe a tropical flavour is added which gives a great scented taste to the dish.

NUTRITIONAL INFORMATION

Calories . . . . . . .200 Sugars 12g

Protein . . . . .21g Fat 7g

Carbohydrate . . .14g Saturates 1g

10 MINS   15 MINS

SERVES 4

INGREDIENTS

175 g/6 oz carrots

2 tbsp vegetable oil

1 red onion, sliced

1 red (bell) pepper, deseeded
   and sliced

1 green (bell) pepper, deseeded
   and sliced

450 g/1 lb skinless cod fillet

1 ripe mango

1 tsp cornflour (cornstarch)

1 tbsp soy sauce

100 ml/3½ fl oz/1⅓ cups tropical
   fruit juice

1 tbsp lime juice

1 tbsp chopped fresh coriander (cilantro),
   to garnish

1 Using a sharp knife, slice the carrots into thin sticks.

2 Heat the oil in a preheated wok and stir-fry the onion, carrots and (bell) peppers for 5 minutes.

3 Using a sharp knife, cut the cod into small cubes. Peel the mango, then carefully remove the flesh from the centre stone. Cut the flesh into thin slices.

4 Add the cod and mango to the wok and stir-fry for a further 4–5 minutes, or until the fish is cooked through. Be careful not to break the fish up.

5 Mix together the cornflour (cornstarch), soy sauce, fruit juice and lime juice. Pour the mixture into the wok and stir until the mixture bubbles and the juices thicken. Scatter with coriander (cilantro) and serve immediately.

 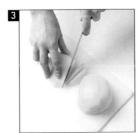 

VARIATION

You can use paw-paw (papaya) as an alternative to the mango, if you prefer.

Scallops in Ginger Sauce

Scallops are both attractive and delicious. Cooked with ginger and orange, this dish is perfect served with plain rice.

NUTRITIONAL INFORMATION

Calories 216   Sugars 4g
Protein . . . . .30g   Fat 8g
Carbohydrate . . . .8g   Saturates 1g

5 MINS   10 MINS

SERVES 4

INGREDIENTS

2 tbsp vegetable oil

450 g/1 lb scallops, cleaned and halved

2.5-cm/1-inch piece fresh root ginger, finely chopped

3 garlic cloves, crushed

2 leeks, shredded

75 g/2¾oz/¾ cup shelled peas

125 g/4½ oz canned bamboo shoots, drained and rinsed

2 tbsp light soy sauce

2 tbsp unsweetened orange juice

1 tsp caster (superfine) sugar

orange zest, to garnish

1 Heat the vegetable oil in a preheated wok or large frying pan (skillet). Add the scallops and stir-fry for 1–2 minutes. Remove the scallops from the wok with a slotted spoon, keep warm and set aside until required.

2 Add the ginger and garlic to the wok and stir-fry for 30 seconds. Stir in the leeks and peas and cook, stirring, for a further 2 minutes.

3 Add the bamboo shoots and return the scallops to the wok. Stir gently to mix without breaking up the scallops.

4 Stir in the soy sauce, orange juice and caster (superfine) sugar and cook for 1–2 minutes.

5 Transfer the stir-fry to a serving dish, garnish with the orange zest and serve immediately.

COOK'S TIP

The edible parts of a scallop are the round white muscle and the orange and white coral or roe. The frilly skirt surrounding the muscle – the gills and mantle – may be used for making shellfish stock. All other parts should be discarded.

Spiced Scallops

Scallops are available both fresh and frozen. Make sure they are completely defrosted before cooking.

NUTRITIONAL INFORMATION

Calories	276	Sugar	.........6g
Protein	........25g	Fat	..........15g
Carbohydrate	....8g	Saturates	.......2g

10 MINS   10 MINS

SERVES 4

I N G R E D I E N T S

12 large scallops with coral attached, defrosted if frozen, or 350 g/ 12 oz small scallops without coral, defrosted

4 tbsp sunflower oil

4–6 spring onions (scallions), thinly sliced diagonally

1 garlic clove, crushed

2.5 cm/1 inch ginger root, finely chopped

250 g/9 oz mangetout (snow peas)

125 g/4½ oz button or closed cup mushrooms, sliced

2 tbsp sherry

2 tbsp soy sauce

1 tbsp clear honey

¼ tsp ground allspice

salt and pepper

1 tbsp sesame seeds, toasted

1 Wash and dry the scallops, discarding any black pieces and detach the corals, if using.

2 Slice each scallop into 3–4 pieces and if the corals are large halve them.

3 Heat 2 tablespoons of the sunflower oil in a preheated wok or large, heavy-based frying pan (skillet), swirling it around until really hot.

4 Add the spring onions (scallions), garlic and ginger to the wok or frying pan (skillet) and stir-fry for about 1 minute.

5 Add the mangetout (snow peas) to the wok and continue to cook for a further 2–3 minutes, stirring continuously. Remove to a bowl and set aside.

6 Add the remaining sunflower oil to the wok and when really hot add the scallops and corals and stir-fry for a couple of minutes.

7 Add the mushrooms and continue to cook for a further minute or so.

8 Add the sherry, soy sauce, honey and allspice to the wok, with salt and pepper to taste. Mix thoroughly, then return the mangetout (snow peas) mixture to the wok.

9 Season well with salt and pepper and toss together over a high heat for a minute or so until piping hot. Serve the scallops and vegetables immediately, sprinkled with sesame seeds.

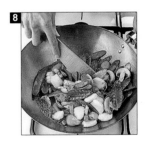

Salmon with Pineapple

Presentation plays a major part in Chinese cooking and this dish demonstrates this perfectly with the wonderful combination of colours.

NUTRITIONAL INFORMATION

Calories ....347 Sugars 12g
Protein ....24g Fat 20g
Carbohydrate ...16g Saturates 3g

 10 MINS   15 MINS

SERVES 4

I N G R E D I E N T S

2 tbsp sunflower oil

1 red onion, sliced

1 orange (bell) pepper, deseeded and sliced

1 green (bell) pepper, deseeded and sliced

100 g/3½ oz/1 cup baby corn cobs

450 g/1 lb salmon fillet, skin removed

1 tbsp paprika

225 g/8 oz can cubed pineapple, drained

100 g/3½ oz/1 cup bean sprouts

2 tbsp tomato ketchup (catsup)

2 tbsp soy sauce

2 tbsp medium sherry

1 tsp cornflour (cornstarch)

1 Cut each baby corn in half. Heat the oil in a large preheated wok. Add the onion, (bell) peppers and baby corn cobs to the wok and stir-fry for 5 minutes.

2 Rinse the salmon fillet under cold running water and pat dry with absorbent kitchen paper (paper towels).

3 Cut the salmon flesh into thin strips and place in a large bowl. Sprinkle with the paprika and toss well to coat.

4 Add the salmon to the wok together with the pineapple and stir-fry for a further 2–3 minutes or until the fish is tender.

5 Add the bean sprouts to the wok and toss well.

6 Mix together the tomato ketchup (catsup), soy sauce, sherry and cornflour (cornstarch). Add to the wok and cook until the juices start to thicken. Transfer to warm serving plates and serve immediately.

VARIATION

You can use trout fillets instead of the salmon as an alternative, if you prefer.

Prawns (Shrimp) with Ginger

Crispy ginger is a wonderful garnish which offsets the spicy prawns (shrimp) both visually and in flavour.

NUTRITIONAL INFORMATION

Calories 229	Sugars 7g
Protein 29g	Fat 8g
Carbohydrate ...10g	Saturates 1g

 10 MINS   15 MINS

SERVES 4

INGREDIENTS

5 cm/2 inch piece fresh root ginger

oil, for frying

1 onion, diced

225 g/8 oz carrots, diced

100 g/3½ oz/½ cup frozen peas

100 g/3½ oz/1 cup bean sprouts

450 g/1 lb peeled king prawns (shrimp)

1 tsp Chinese five-spice powder

1 tbsp tomato purée (paste)

1 tbsp soy sauce

1 Using a sharp knife, peel the ginger and slice it into very thin sticks.

2 Heat about 2.5 cm/1 inch of oil in a large preheated wok. Add the ginger and stir-fry for 1 minute or until the ginger is crispy. Remove the ginger with a slotted spoon and leave to drain on absorbent kitchen paper (paper towels).

3 Drain all of the oil from the wok except for about 2 tablespoons. Add the onions and carrots to the wok and stir-fry for 5 minutes. Add the peas and bean sprouts and stir-fry for 2 minutes.

4 Rinse the prawns (shrimp) under cold running water and pat dry with absorbent kitchen paper (paper towels).

5 Combine the five-spice, tomato purée (paste) and soy sauce. Brush the mixture over the prawns (shrimp).

6 Add the prawns (shrimp) to the wok and stir-fry for a further 2 minutes, or until the prawns (shrimp) are completely cooked through. Transfer the prawn (shrimp) mixture to a warm serving bowl and top with the reserved crispy ginger. Serve immediately.

VARIATION

Use slices of white fish instead of the prawns (shrimp) as an alternative, if you wish.

Spicy Mushrooms

A mixture of mushrooms, common in Western cooking, have been used in this recipe for a richly flavoured dish.

NUTRITIONAL INFORMATION

Calories 103   Sugars 4g
Protein . . . . .3g   Fat 8g
Carbohydrate . . . .5g   Saturates 2g

5 MINS   10 MINS

SERVES 4

INGREDIENTS

2 tbsp peanut oil

2 garlic cloves, crushed

3 spring onions (scallions), chopped

300 g/10½ oz button mushrooms

2 large open-cap mushrooms, sliced

125 g/4½ oz oyster mushrooms

1 tsp chilli sauce

1 tbsp dark soy sauce

1 tbsp hoisin sauce

1 tbsp wine vinegar

½ tsp ground Szechuan pepper

1 tbsp dark brown sugar

1 tsp sesame oil

chopped parsley, to garnish

1 Heat the peanut oil in a preheated wok or large frying pan (skillet) until almost smoking.

2 Reduce the heat slightly, add the garlic and spring onions (scallions) to the wok or frying pan (skillet) and stir-fry for 30 seconds.

3 Add all the mushrooms to the wok, together with the chilli sauce, dark soy sauce, hoisin sauce, wine vinegar, ground Szechuan pepper and dark brown sugar and stir-fry for 4–5 minutes, or until the mushrooms are cooked through. Stir constantly to prevent the mixture sticking to the base of the wok.

4 Sprinkle the sesame oil on top of the mixture in the wok. Transfer to a warm serving dish, garnish with parsley and serve immediately.

COOK'S TIP

If Chinese dried mushrooms are available, add a small quantity to this dish for texture. Wood (tree) ears are widely used and are available dried from Chinese food stores. They should be rinsed, soaked in warm water for 20 minutes and rinsed again before use.

Stir-Fried Seasonal Vegetables

When selecting different fresh vegetables for this dish, bear in mind that there should always be a contrast in colour as well as texture.

NUTRITIONAL INFORMATION

Calories	108	Sugars	. . . . .3g
Protein	. . . . .3g	Fat	. . . . .9g
Carbohydrate	. . . .4g	Saturates	. . . . . . .1g

15 MINS   10 MINS

SERVES 4

INGREDIENTS

1 medium red (bell) pepper, cored and seeded

125 g/4½ oz courgettes (zucchini)

125 g/4½ oz cauliflower

125 g/4½ oz French (green) beans

3 tbsp vegetable oil

a few small slices ginger root

½ tsp salt

½ tsp sugar

Chinese stock or water

1 tbsp light soy sauce

a few drops of sesame oil (optional)

VARIATION

Almost any vegetables could be used in this dish but make sure there is a good variety of colour, and always include several crisp vegetables such as carrots or mangetout (snow peas).

1 Using a sharp knife or cleaver, cut the red (bell) pepper into small squares. Thinly slice the courgettes (zucchini). Trim the cauliflower and divide into small florets, discarding any thick stems. Make sure the vegetables are cut into roughly similar shapes and sizes to ensure even cooking.

2 Top and tail the French (green) beans, then cut them in half.

3 Heat the vegetable oil in a pre-heated wok or large frying pan (skillet).

4 Add the prepared vegetables to the wok and stir-fry with the ginger for about 2 minutes.

5 Add the salt and sugar to the wok or frying pan (skillet), and continue to stir-fry for 1–2 minutes, adding a little Chinese stock or water if the vegetables appear to be too dry. Do not add liquid unless necessary.

6 Add the light soy sauce and sesame oil (if using) and stir well to lightly coat the vegetables.

7 Transfer the stir-fried vegetables to a warm serving dish and serve immediately.

Potato Stir-Fry

In this sweet and sour dish, tender vegetables are simply stir-fried with spices and coconut milk, and flavoured with lime.

NUTRITIONAL INFORMATION

Calories 138	Sugars 5g
Protein 2g	Fat 6g
Carbohydrate ...20g	Saturates 1g

 10 MINS   20 MINS

SERVES 4

I N G R E D I E N T S

4 waxy potatoes

2 tbsp vegetable oil

1 yellow (bell) pepper, diced

1 red (bell) pepper, diced

1 carrot, cut into matchstick strips

1 courgette (zucchini), cut into
    matchstick strips

2 garlic cloves, crushed

1 red chilli, sliced

1 bunch spring onions (scallions),
    halved lengthways

8 tbsp coconut milk

1 tsp chopped lemon grass

2 tsp lime juice

finely grated rind of 1 lime

1 tbsp chopped fresh coriander
    (cilantro)

1 Using a sharp knife, cut the potatoes into small dice.

2 Bring a large saucepan of water to the boil and cook the diced potatoes for 5 minutes. Drain thoroughly.

3 Heat the vegetable oil in a wok or large frying pan (skillet), swirling the oil around the base of the wok until it is really hot.

4 Add the potatoes, diced (bell) peppers, carrot, courgette (zucchini), garlic and chilli to the wok and stir-fry the vegetables for 2–3 minutes.

5 Stir in the spring onions, (scallions), coconut milk, chopped lemon grass and lime juice and stir-fry the mixture for a further 5 minutes.

6 Add the lime rind and coriander (cilantro) and stir-fry for 1 minute. Serve hot.

COOK'S TIP

Check that the potatoes are not overcooked in step 2, otherwise the potato pieces will disintegrate when they are stir-fried in the wok.

Ginger & Orange Broccoli

Thinly sliced broccoli florets are lightly stir-fried and served in a ginger and orange sauce.

NUTRITIONAL INFORMATION

Calories 133	Sugars 6g	
Protein 9g	Fat 7g	
Carbohydrate ...10g	Saturates 1g	

 5 MINS   10 MINS

SERVES 4

INGREDIENTS

750 g/1 lb 10 oz broccoli

2 thin slices ginger root

2 garlic cloves

1 orange

2 tsp cornflour (cornstarch)

1 tbsp light soy sauce

½ tsp sugar

2 tbsp vegetable oil

1 Divide the broccoli into small florets. Peel the stems, using a vegetable peeler, and then cut the stems into thin slices, using a sharp knife.

2 Cut the ginger root into matchsticks and slice the garlic.

3 Peel 2 long strips of zest from the orange and cut into thin strips. Place the strips in a bowl, cover with cold water and set aside.

4 Squeeze the juice from the orange and mix with the cornflour (cornstarch), light soy sauce, sugar and 4 tablespoons water.

5 Heat the vegetable oil in a wok or large frying pan (skillet). Add the broccoli stem slices and stir-fry for 2 minutes.

6 Add the ginger root slices, garlic and broccoli florets, and stir-fry for a further 3 minutes.

7 Stir the orange sauce mixture into the wok and cook, stirring constantly, until the sauce has thickened and coated the broccoli.

8 Drain the reserved orange rind and stir into the wok before serving.

VARIATION

This dish could be made with cauliflower, if you prefer, or a mixture of cauliflower and broccoli.

Carrot & Orange Stir-Fry

Carrots and oranges have long been combined in Oriental cooking, the orange juice bringing out the sweetness of the carrots.

NUTRITIONAL INFORMATION

Calories 341   Sugars 26g
Protein . . . . .10g   Fat 21g
Carbohydrate . . .28g   Saturates 4g

10 MINS   10 MINS

SERVES 4

INGREDIENTS

2 tbsp sunflower oil

450 g/1 lb carrots, grated

225 g/8 oz leeks, shredded

2 oranges, peeled and segmented

2 tbsp tomato ketchup (catsup)

1 tbsp demerara (brown crystal) sugar

2 tbsp light soy sauce

100 g/3½ oz/½ cup chopped peanuts

VARIATION

You could use pineapple instead of orange, if you prefer. If using canned pineapple, make sure that it is in natural juice not syrup as it will spoil the fresh taste of this dish.

1 Heat the sunflower oil in a large preheated wok.

2 Add the grated carrot and leeks to the wok and stir-fry for 2–3 minutes, or until the vegetables have just softened.

3 Add the orange segments to the wok and heat through gently, ensuring that you do not break up the orange segments as you stir the mixture.

4 Mix the tomato ketchup (catsup), demerara (brown crystal) sugar and soy sauce together in a small bowl.

5 Add the tomato and sugar mixture to the wok and stir-fry for a further 2 minutes.

6 Transfer the stir-fry to warm serving bowls and scatter with the chopped peanuts. Serve immediately.

Vegetable Stir-Fry with Eggs

Known as Gado Gado in China, this is a true classic which never fades from popularity. A delicious warm salad with a peanut sauce.

NUTRITIONAL INFORMATION

Calories	269	Sugars 12g
Protein	........12g	Fat 19g
Carbohydrate	...14g	Saturates 3g

 10 MINS   15 MINS

SERVES 4

INGREDIENTS

2 eggs

225 g/8 oz carrots

350 g/12 oz white cabbage

2 tbsp vegetable oil

1 red (bell) pepper, deseeded and thinly sliced

150 g/5½ oz/1½ cups bean sprouts

1 tbsp tomato ketchup (catsup)

2 tbsp soy sauce

75 g/2¾ oz/⅓ cup salted peanuts, chopped

1 Bring a small saucepan of water to the boil. Add the eggs to the pan and cook for about 7 minutes. Remove the eggs from the pan and leave to cool under cold running water for 1 minute. Peel the shell from the eggs and then cut the eggs into quarters.

2 Peel and coarsley grate the carrots.

3 Remove any outer leaves from the white cabbage and cut out the stem, then shred the leaves very finely, either with a sharp knife or by using the fine slicing blade on a food processor.

4 Heat the vegetable oil in a large preheated wok or large frying pan (skillet).

5 Add the carrots, white cabbage and (bell) pepper to the wok and stir-fry for 3 minutes.

6 Add the bean sprouts to the wok and stir-fry for 2 minutes.

7 Combine the tomato ketchup (catsup) and soy sauce in a small bowl and add to the wok or frying pan (skillet).

8 Add the chopped peanuts to the wok and stir-fry for 1 minute.

9 Transfer the stir-fry to warm serving plates and garnish with the hard-boiled (hard-cooked) egg quarters. Serve immediately.

COOK'S TIP

The eggs are cooled in cold water immediately after cooking in order to prevent the egg yolk blackening around the edges.

Spinach with Mushrooms

For best results, use straw mushrooms, available in cans from oriental shops. If these are unavailable, use button mushrooms instead.

NUTRITIONAL INFORMATION

Calories 201	Sugars 8g
Protein 7g	Fat 15g
Carbohydrate . . .10g	Saturates 2g

5 MINS   10 MINS

SERVES 4

I N G R E D I E N T S

25 g/1 oz/¼ cup pine kernels (nuts)

500 g/1 lb 2 oz fresh spinach leaves

1 red onion

2 garlic cloves

3 tbsp vegetable oil

425 g/15 oz can straw mushrooms, drained

25 g/1 oz/3 tbsp raisins

2 tbsp soy sauce

salt

1 Heat a wok or large, heavy-based frying pan (skillet).

2 Dry-fry the pine kernels (nuts) in the wok until lightly browned. Remove with a perforated spoon and set aside until required.

3 Wash the spinach thoroughly, picking the leaves over and removing long stalks. Drain thoroughly and pat dry with absorbent kitchen paper (paper towels).

4 Using a sharp knife, slice the red onion and the garlic.

5 Heat the vegetable oil in the wok or frying pan (skillet). Add the onion and garlic slices and stir-fry for 1 minute until slightly softened.

6 Add the spinach and mushrooms, and continue to stir-fry until the leaves have wilted. Drain off any excess liquid.

7 Stir in the raisins, reserved pine kernels (nuts) and soy sauce. Stir-fry until thoroughly heated and all the ingredients are well combined.

8 Season to taste with salt, transfer to a warm serving dish and serve.

COOK'S TIP

Soak the raisins in 2 tablespoons dry sherry before using. This helps to plump them up as well as adding extra flavour to the stir-fry.

Quorn & Vegetable Stir-Fry

Quorn, like tofu (bean curd), absorbs all of the flavours in a dish, making it ideal for this recipe which is packed with classic Chinese flavourings.

NUTRITIONAL INFORMATION

Calories 167   Sugars 8g
Protein ....12g   Fat 9g
Carbohydrate ...10g   Saturates 1g

 30 MINS   10 MINS

SERVES 4

I N G R E D I E N T S

1 tbsp grated fresh root ginger

1 tsp ground ginger

1 tbsp tomato purée (paste)

2 tbsp sunflower oil

1 clove garlic, crushed

2 tbsp soy sauce

350 g/12 oz Quorn or soya cubes

225 g/8 oz carrots, sliced

100 g/3½ oz green beans, sliced

4 stalks celery, sliced

1 red (bell) pepper, deseeded and sliced

boiled rice, to serve

COOK'S TIP

Ginger root will keep for several weeks in a cool, dry place. Ginger root can also be kept frozen – break off lumps as needed.

1 Place the grated fresh root ginger, ground ginger, tomato purée (paste), 1 tablespoon of the sunflower oil, garlic, soy sauce and Quorn or soya cubes in a large bowl. Mix well to combine, stirring carefully so that you don't break up the Quorn or soya cubes. Cover and leave to marinate for 20 minutes.

2 Heat the remaining sunflower oil in a large preheated wok.

3 Add the marinated Quorn mixture to the wok and stir-fry for about 2 minutes.

4 Add the carrots, green beans, celery and red (bell) pepper to the wok and stir-fry for a further 5 minutes.

5 Transfer the stir-fry to warm serving dishes and serve immediately with freshly cooked boiled rice.

Honey-Fried Spinach

This stir-fry is the perfect accompaniment to tofu (bean curd) dishes, and it is so quick and simple to make.

NUTRITIONAL INFORMATION

Calories ....146 Sugars 9g
Protein ....4g Fat 9g
Carbohydrate ...10g Saturates 2g

5 MINS   15 MINS

SERVES 4

I N G R E D I E N T S

4 spring onions (scallions)

3 tbsp groundnut oil

350 g/12 oz shiitake mushrooms, sliced

2 cloves garlic, crushed

350 g/12 oz baby leaf spinach

2 tbsp dry sherry

2 tbsp clear honey

1 Using a sharp knife, slice the spring onions (scallions).

2 Heat the groundnut oil in a large preheated wok or heavy-based frying pan (skillet).

3 Add the shiitake mushrooms to the wok and stir-fry for about 5 minutes, or until the mushrooms have softened.

COOK'S TIP

Single-flower honey has a better, more individual flavour than blended honey. Acacia honey is typically Chinese, but you could also try clover, lemon blossom, lime flower or orange blossom.

4 Stir the crushed garlic into the wok or frying pan (skillet).

5 Add the baby leaf spinach to the wok or pan and stir-fry for a further 2–3 minutes, or until the spinach leaves have just wilted.

6 Mix together the dry sherry and clear honey in a small bowl until well combined. Drizzle the sherry and honey mixture over the spinach and heat through, stirring to coat the spinach leaves thoroughly in the mixture.

7 Transfer the stir-fry to warm serving dishes, scatter with the chopped spring onions (scallions) and serve immediately.

Chinese Fried Vegetables

The Chinese are known for their colourful, crisp vegetables, quickly stir-fried. In this recipe, they are tossed in a tasty soy and hoisin sauce.

NUTRITIONAL INFORMATION

Calories 137	Sugars 7g
Protein 8g	Fat 7g
Carbohydrate ...10g	Saturates 11g

5 MINS   10 MINS

SERVES 4

INGREDIENTS

2 tbsp peanut oil

350 g/12 oz broccoli florets

1 tbsp chopped fresh root ginger

2 onions, cut into 8

3 celery sticks, sliced

175 g/6 oz baby spinach

125 g/4½ oz mangetout (snow peas)

6 spring onions (scallions), quartered

2 garlic cloves, crushed

2 tbsp light soy sauce

2 tsp caster (superfine) sugar

2 tbsp dry sherry

1 tbsp hoisin sauce

150 ml/¼ pint/⅔ cup vegetable stock

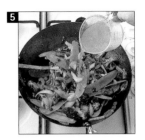

1 Heat the peanut oil in a preheated wok until it is almost smoking.

2 Add the broccoli florets, chopped root ginger, onions and celery to the wok and stir-fry for 1 minute.

3 Add the spinach, mangetout (snow peas), spring onions (scallions) and garlic and stir-fry for 3–4 minutes.

4 Mix together the soy sauce, caster (superfine) sugar, sherry, hoisin sauce and vegetable stock.

5 Pour the stock mixture into the wok, mixing well to coat the vegetables.

6 Cover the wok and cook over a medium heat for 2–3 minutes, or until the vegetables are cooked through, but still crisp.

7 Transfer the Chinese fried vegetables to a warm serving dish and serve immediately.

COOK'S TIP

You could use this mixture to fill Chinese pancakes. They are available from Chinese food stores and can be reheated in a steamer in 2–3 minutes.

Butternut Squash Stir-Fry

Butternut squash is as its name suggests, deliciously buttery and nutty in flavour. If the squash is not in season, use sweet potatoes instead.

NUTRITIONAL INFORMATION

Calories	301	Sugars	4g
Protein	9g	Fat	22g
Carbohydrate	19g	Saturates	4g

5 MINS   25 MINS

SERVES 4

INGREDIENTS

1 kg/2 lb 4 oz butternut squash, peeled

3 tbsp groundnut oil

1 onion, sliced

2 cloves garlic, crushed

1 tsp coriander seeds

1 tsp cumin seeds

2 tbsp chopped coriander (cilantro)

150 ml/¼ pint/⅔ cup coconut milk

100 ml/3½ fl oz/½ cup water

100 g/3½ oz/⅓ cup salted cashew nuts

TO GARNISH

freshly grated lime zest

fresh coriander (cilantro)

lime wedges

1 Using a sharp knife, slice the butternut squash into small, bite-sized cubes.

2 Heat the groundnut oil in a large preheated wok.

3 Add the butternut squash, onion and garlic to the wok and stir-fry for 5 minutes.

4 Stir in the coriander seeds, cumin seeds and fresh coriander (cilantro) and stir-fry for 1 minute.

5 Add the coconut milk and water to the wok and bring to the boil. Cover the wok and leave to simmer for 10–15 minutes, or until the squash is tender.

6 Add the cashew nuts and stir to combine.

7 Transfer to warm serving dishes and garnish with freshly grated lime zest, fresh coriander (cilantro) and lime wedges. Serve hot.

COOK'S TIP

If you do not have coconut milk, grate some creamed coconut into the dish with the water in step 5.

Green Stir-Fry

The basis of this recipe is pak choi, also known as bok choy or Chinese greens. If unavailable, use Swiss chard or Savoy cabbage instead.

NUTRITIONAL INFORMATION

Calories 107   Sugars 6g
Protein . . . . .4g   Fat 8g
Carbohydrate . . . .6g   Saturates 1g

 5 MINS   10 MINS

SERVES 4

I N G R E D I E N T S

2 tbsp peanut oil

2 garlic cloves, crushed

½ tsp ground star anise

1 tsp salt

350 g/12 oz pak choi, shredded

225 g/8 oz baby spinach

25 g/1 oz mangetout (snow peas)

1 celery stick, sliced

1 green (bell) pepper, seeded and sliced

50 ml/2 fl oz/¼ cup vegetable stock

1 tsp sesame oil

1 Heat the peanut oil in a preheated wok or large frying pan (skillet), swirling the oil around the base of the wok until it is really hot.

2 Add the crushed garlic to the wok or frying pan (skillet) and stir-fry for about 30 seconds.

3 Stir in the ground star anise, salt, shredded pak choi, spinach, mangetout (snow peas), celery and green (bell) pepper and stir-fry for 3–4 minutes.

4 Add the vegetable stock, cover the wok and cook for 3–4 minutes.

5 Remove the lid from the wok and stir in the sesame oil. Mix thoroughly to combine all the ingredients.

6 Transfer the green vegetable stir-fry to a warm serving dish and serve.

COOK'S TIP

Star anise is an important ingredient in Chinese cuisine. The attractive star-shaped pods are often used whole to add a decorative garnish to dishes. The flavour is similar to liquorice, but with spicy undertones and is quite strong.

Vegetable Stir-Fry

A range of delicious flavours are captured in this simple recipe which is ideal if you are in a hurry.

NUTRITIONAL INFORMATION

Calories 138   Sugars 5g
Protein ....3g   Fat 12g
Carbohydrate ....5g   Saturates 2g

5 MINS   25 MINS

SERVES 4

I N G R E D I E N T S

3 tbsp vegetable oil

8 baby onions, halved

1 aubergine (eggplant), cubed

225 g/8 oz courgettes (zucchini), sliced

225 g/8 oz open-cap mushrooms, halved

2 cloves garlic, crushed

400 g/14 oz can chopped tomatoes

2 tbsp sundried tomato purée (paste)

2 tbsp soy sauce

1 tsp sesame oil

1 tbsp Chinese rice wine or dry sherry

freshly ground black pepper

fresh basil leaves, to garnish

1 Heat the vegetable oil in a large preheated wok or frying pan (skillet).

2 Add the baby onions and aubergine (eggplant) to the wok or frying pan (skillet) and stir-fry for 5 minutes, or until the vegetables are golden and just beginning to soften.

3 Add the sliced courgettes (zucchini), mushrooms, garlic, chopped tomatoes and tomato purée (paste) to the wok and stir-fry for about 5 minutes. Reduce the heat and leave to simmer for 10 minutes, or until the vegetables are tender.

4 Add the soy sauce, sesame oil and rice wine or sherry to the wok, bring back to the boil and cook for 1 minute.

5 Season the vegetable stir-fry with freshly ground black pepper and scatter with fresh basil leaves. Serve immediately.

COOK'S TIP

Basil has a very strong flavour which is perfect with vegetables and Chinese flavourings. Instead of using basil simply as a garnish in this dish, try adding a handful of fresh basil leaves to the stir-fry in step 4.

Stir-Fried Spinach

This is an easy recipe to make as a quick accompaniment to a main course. The water chestnuts give a delicious crunch to the greens.

NUTRITIONAL INFORMATION

Calories 85   Sugars 2g
Protein ....4g   Fat 4g
Carbohydrate ....9g   Saturates 1g

 5 MINS   10 MINS

SERVES 4

I N G R E D I E N T S

1 tbsp sunflower oil

1 garlic clove, halved

2 spring onions (scallions),
   sliced finely

225 g/8 oz can water
   chestnuts, drained and sliced
   finely (optional)

500 g/1 lb 2 oz spinach, any tough
   stalks removed

1 tsp sherry vinegar

1 tsp light soy sauce

pepper

1 Heat the sunflower oil in a wok or large, heavy frying pan (skillet) over a high heat, swirling the oil around the base of the wok until it is really hot.

2 Add the halved garlic clove and cook, stirring, for 1 minute. If the garlic should brown, remove it immediately.

3 Add the finely sliced spring onions (scallions) and water chestnuts, if using, and stir for 2–3 minutes.

4 Add the spinach leaves and stir into the wok.

5 Add the sherry vinegar, soy sauce and a sprinkling of pepper. Cook, stirring, until the spinach is tender. Remove the garlic.

6 Using a slotted spoon, drain off the excess liquid from the wok and serve the stir-fried greens immediately.

COOK'S TIP

Several types of oriental greens (for example, choi sam and pak choi) are widely available and any of these can be successfully substituted for the spinach.

Stir-Fried Japanese Noodles

This quick dish is an ideal lunchtime meal, packed with whatever mixture of mushrooms you like in a sweet sauce.

NUTRITIONAL INFORMATION

Calories	379	Sugars	.........8g
Protein	........12g	Fat	..........13g
Carbohydrate	...53g	Saturates	.......3g

15 MINS   15 MINS

SERVES 4

INGREDIENTS

225 g/8 oz Japanese egg noodles

2 tbsp sunflower oil

1 red onion, sliced

1 garlic clove, crushed

500 g/1 lb 2 oz mixed mushrooms, such as
    shiitake, oyster, brown cap

350 g/12 oz pak choi

2 tbsp sweet sherry

6 tbsp soy sauce

4 spring onions (scallions), sliced

1 tbsp toasted sesame seeds

1 Place the egg noodles in a large bowl. Pour over enough boiling water to cover and leave to soak for 10 minutes.

2 Heat the sunflower oil in a large preheated wok.

3 Add the red onion and garlic to the wok and stir-fry for 2–3 minutes, or until softened.

4 Add the mushrooms to the wok and stir-fry for about 5 minutes, or until the mushrooms have softened.

5 Drain the Japanese egg noodles thoroughly and set aside.

6 Add the the pak choi, noodles, sweet sherry and soy sauce to the wok. Toss all of the ingredients together to mix well and stir-fry for 2–3 minutes, or until the liquid is just bubbling.

7 Transfer the mushroom noodles to warm serving bowls and scatter with sliced spring onions (scallions) and toasted sesame seeds. Serve immediately.

COOK'S TIP

The variety of mushrooms in supermarkets has greatly improved and a good mixture should be easily obtainable. If not, use the more common button and flat mushrooms.

Vegetable Sesame Stir-Fry

Sesame seeds add a delicious flavour to any recipe and are particularly good with vegetables in this soy and rice wine or sherry sauce.

NUTRITIONAL INFORMATION

Calories 118   Sugars 2g
Protein . . . . .3g   Fat 9g
Carbohydrate . . . .5g   Saturates 1g

 5 MINS   10 MINS

SERVES 4

I N G R E D I E N T S

2 tbsp vegetable oil

3 garlic cloves, crushed

1 tbsp sesame seeds,
   plus extra to garnish

2 celery sticks, sliced

2 baby corn cobs, sliced

60 g/2 oz button mushrooms

1 leek, sliced

1 courgette (zucchini), sliced

1 small red (bell) pepper, sliced

1 fresh green chilli, sliced

60 g/2 oz Chinese leaves (cabbage),
   shredded

rice or noodles, to serve

S A U C E

½ tsp Chinese curry powder

2 tbsp light soy sauce

1 tbsp Chinese rice wine or dry sherry

1 tsp sesame oil

1 tsp cornflour (cornstarch)

4 tbsp water

1 Heat the vegetable oil in a preheated wok or heavy-based frying pan (skillet), swirling the oil around the base of the wok until it is almost smoking.

2 Lower the heat slightly, add the garlic and sesame seeds and stir-fry for 30 seconds.

3 Add the celery, baby corn cobs, mushrooms, leek, courgette (zucchini), (bell) pepper, chilli and Chinese leaves (cabbage) and stir-fry for 4–5 minutes, until the vegetables are beginning to soften.

4 To make the sauce, mix together the Chinese curry powder, light soy sauce, Chinese rice wine or dry sherry, sesame oil, cornflour (cornstarch) and water.

5 Stir the sauce mixture into the wok until well combined with the other ingredients.

6 Bring to the boil and cook, stirring constantly, until the sauce thickens and clears.

7 Cook for 1 minute, spoon into a warm serving dish and garnish with sesame seeds. Serve the vegetable sesame stir-fry immediately with rice or noodles.

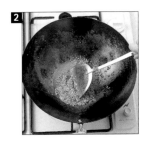

Winter Vegetable Stir-Fry

Ordinary winter vegetables are given extraordinary treatment in this lively stir-fry, just the thing for perking up jaded palates.

NUTRITIONAL INFORMATION

Calories 175   Sugars 7g
Protein . . . . .6g   Fat 13g
Carbohydrate . . . .9g   Saturates 2g

5 MINS   10 MINS

SERVES 4

INGREDIENTS

3 tbsp sesame oil

25 g/1 oz/¼ cup blanched almonds

1 large carrot, cut into thin strips

1 large turnip, cut into thin strips

1 onion, sliced finely

1 garlic clove, crushed

3 celery sticks, sliced finely

125 g/4½ oz Brussels sprouts, trimmed and halved

125 g/4½ oz cauliflower, broken into florets

125 g/4½ oz/2 cups white cabbage, shredded

2 tsp sesame seeds

1 tsp grated fresh root ginger

½ tsp medium chilli powder

1 tbsp chopped fresh coriander (cilantro)

1 tbsp light soy sauce

salt and pepper

sprigs of fresh coriander (cilantro), to garnish

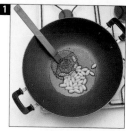  

1 Heat the oil in a wok or large frying pan (skillet). Stir-fry the almonds until lightly browned, then lift them out and drain on kitchen paper (paper towels).

2 Add all the vegetables to the wok or frying pan (skillet), except for the cabbage. Stir-fry the vegetables briskly for 3–4 minutes.

3 Add the cabbage, sesame seeds, ginger and chilli powder and cook, stirring, for 2 minutes. Season to taste.

4 Add the chopped coriander (cilantro), soy sauce and almonds, stirring gently to mix. Serve the vegetables, garnished with coriander (cilantro) sprigs.

COOK'S TIP

As well as adding protein, vitamins and useful fats to the diet, nuts and seeds add important flavour and texture to vegetarian meals. Sesame seeds are also a good source of vitamin E.

Vegetable & Nut Stir-Fry

A colourful selection of vegetables are stir-fried in a creamy peanut sauce and sprinkled with nuts to serve.

NUTRITIONAL INFORMATION

Calories 325	Sugars 6g	
Protein 11g	Fat 21g	
Carbohydrate ...26g	Saturates 4g	

 10 MINS 15 MINS

SERVES 4

INGREDIENTS

3 tbsp crunchy peanut butter

150 ml/¼ pint/⅔ cup water

1 tbsp soy sauce

1 tsp sugar

1 carrot

½ red onion

4 baby courgettes (zucchini)

1 red (bell) pepper

250 g/9 oz egg thread noodles

25 g/1 oz/¼ cup peanuts, chopped roughly

2 tbsp vegetable oil

1 tsp sesame oil

1 small green chilli, deseeded and sliced thinly

1 garlic clove, sliced thinly

225 g/8 oz can water chestnuts, drained and sliced

175 g/6 oz/3 cups bean sprouts

salt

1 Gradually blend the peanut butter with the water in a small bowl. Stir in the soy sauce and sugar. Set aside.

2 Cut the carrot into thin matchsticks and slice the red onion. Slice the courgettes (zucchini) on the diagonal and cut the (bell) pepper into chunks.

3 Bring a large pan of water to the boil and add the egg noodles. Remove from the heat immediately and leave to stand for 4 minutes, stirring occasionally to separate the noodles.

4 Heat a wok or large frying pan (skillet), add the peanuts and dry-fry until they are beginning to brown. Remove with a perforated spoon and set aside until required.

5 Add the oils to the pan and heat. Add the carrot, onion, courgette (zucchini), (bell) pepper, chilli and garlic, and stir-fry for 2–3 minutes. Add the water chestnuts, bean sprouts and peanut sauce. Bring to the boil and heat thoroughly. Season with salt to taste.

6 Drain the noodles and serve with the vegetable and nut stir-fry. Sprinkle with the reserved peanuts.

Chestnut & Vegetable Stir-Fry

In this colourful stir-fry, vegetables are cooked in a wonderfully aromatic sauce which combines peanuts, chilli, coconut, coriander and turmeric.

NUTRITIONAL INFORMATION

Calories ....446 Sugars 17g
Protein ....14g Fat 25g
Carbohydrate ...42g Saturates 5g

10 MINS   15 MINS

SERVES 4

I N G R E D I E N T S

125 g/4½ oz/1 cup unsalted roasted peanuts

2 tsp hot chilli sauce

175 ml/6 fl oz/¾ cup coconut milk

2 tbsp soy sauce

1 tbsp ground coriander

pinch of ground turmeric

1 tbsp dark muscovado sugar

3 tbsp sesame oil

3–4 shallots, finely sliced

1 garlic clove, finely sliced

1–2 red chillies, deseeded and finely chopped

1 large carrot, cut into fine strips

1 yellow and 1 red (bell) pepper, sliced

1 courgette (zucchini), cut into fine strips

125 g/4½ oz sugar-snap peas, trimmed

7.5-cm/3-inch piece cucumber, cut into strips

250 g/9 oz oyster mushrooms,

250 g/9 oz canned chestnuts, drained

2 tsp grated ginger root

finely grated rind and juice of 1 lime

1 tbsp chopped fresh coriander (cilantro)

salt and pepper

slices of lime, to garnish

1 To make the peanut sauce, grind the peanuts in a blender, or chop very finely. Put into a small pan with the hot chilli sauce, coconut milk, soy sauce, ground coriander, ground turmeric and dark muscovado sugar. Heat gently and simmer for 3–4 minutes. Keep warm and set aside until required.

2 Heat the sesame oil in a wok or large frying pan (skillet). Add the shallots, garlic and chillies and stir-fry for 2 minutes.

3 Add the carrot, (bell) peppers, courgette (zucchini) and sugar-snap peas to the wok or pan (skillet) and stir-fry for 2 more minutes.

4 Add the cucumber, mushrooms, chestnuts, ginger, lime rind and juice and fresh coriander (cilantro) to the wok or pan (skillet) and stir-fry briskly for about 5 minutes, or until the vegetables are crisp, yet crunchy.

5 Season to taste with salt and pepper.

6 Divide the stir-fry between four warmed serving plates, and garnish with slices of lime. Transfer the peanut sauce to a serving dish and serve with the vegetables.

Stir-Fried Mixed Vegetables

The Chinese carefully select vegetables to achieve a harmonious balance of contrasting colours and textures.

NUTRITIONAL INFORMATION

Calories 534   Sugars 8g
Protein ....14g   Fat 45g
Carbohydrate ...19g   Saturates 5g

 5 MINS   5 MINS

SERVES 4

INGREDIENTS

60g/2 oz mangetout (snow peas)

1 small carrot

125 g/4½ oz Chinese leaves (cabbage)

60 g/2 oz black or white mushrooms

60 g/2 oz canned bamboo shoots, rinsed and drained

3–4 tbsp vegetable oil

125 g/4½ oz fresh bean sprouts

1 tsp salt

1 tsp sugar

1 tbsp oyster sauce or light soy sauce

a few drops sesame oil (optional)

dip sauce, to serve (optional)

1 Prepare the vegetables: top and tail the mangetout (snow peas), and cut the carrot, Chinese leaves (cabbage), mushrooms and bamboo shoots into roughly the same shape and size as the mangetout (snow peas).

2 Heat the vegetable oil in a preheated wok or large frying pan (skillet) and add the carrot. Stir-fry for a few seconds, then add the mangetout (snow peas) and Chinese leaves (cabbage) and stir-fry for about 1 minute.

3 Add the bean sprouts, mushrooms and bamboo shoots to the wok or frying pan (skillet) and continue to stir-fry for another minute.

4 Add the salt and sugar, continue stirring for another minute, then add the oyster sauce or light soy sauce, blending well.

5 Sprinkle the vegetables with sesame oil (if using) and serve hot or cold, with a dip sauce, if liked.

COOK'S TIP

Oyster sauce is used in many Cantonese dishes. It is worth buying an expensive brand as it will be noticeably better. Good oyster sauce has a rich, almost beefy flavour. Once opened, a bottle of oyster sauce can be kept for months in the refrigerator.

Tofu & Vegetable Stir-Fry

This is a quick dish to prepare, making it ideal as a mid-week supper dish, after a busy day at work!

NUTRITIONAL INFORMATION

Calories 124	Sugars 2g
Protein 6g	Fat 6g
Carbohydrate 11g	Saturates 1g

 5 MINS   25 MINS

SERVES 4

I N G R E D I E N T S

175 g/6 oz/1¼ cups potatoes, cubed

1 tbsp vegetable oil

1 red onion, sliced

225 g/8 oz firm tofu (bean curd), diced

2 courgettes (zucchini), diced

8 canned artichoke hearts, halved

150 ml/¼ pint/⅔ cup passata (sieved tomatoes)

1 tbsp sweet chilli sauce

1 tbsp soy sauce

1 tsp caster (superfine) sugar

2 tbsp chopped basil

salt and pepper

1 Cook the potatoes in a saucepan of boiling water for 10 minutes. Drain thoroughly and set aside until required.

2 Heat the vegetable oil in a wok or large frying pan (skillet) and sauté the red onion for 2 minutes until the onion has softened, stirring.

3 Stir in the diced tofu (bean curd) and courgettes (zucchini) and cook for 3–4 minutes until they begin to brown slightly.

4 Add the cooked potatoes to the wok or frying pan (skillet), stirring to mix.

5 Stir in the artichoke hearts, passata (sieved tomatoes), sweet chilli sauce, soy sauce, sugar and basil.

6 Season to taste with salt and pepper and cook for a further 5 minutes, stirring well.

7 Transfer the tofu (bean curd) and vegetable stir-fry to serving dishes and serve immediately.

COOK'S TIP

Canned artichoke hearts should be drained thoroughly and rinsed before use because they often have salt added.

Mixed Bean Stir-Fry

Any type of canned beans can be used – butter beans, black-eyed beans etc – but rinse under cold water and drain well before use.

NUTRITIONAL INFORMATION

Calories 326   Sugars 16g
Protein . . . . .18g   Fat 7g
Carbohydrate . . .51g   Saturates 1g

10 MINS   10 MINS

SERVES 4

I N G R E D I E N T S

1 x 400 g/14 oz can red kidney beans

1 x 400 g/14 oz can cannellini beans

6 spring onions (scallions)

1 x 200 g/7 oz can pineapple rings or pieces in natural juice, chopped

2 tbsp pineapple juice

3–4 pieces stem ginger

2 tbsp ginger syrup from the jar

thinly pared rind of ½ lime or lemon, cut into julienne strips

2 tbsp lime or lemon juice

2 tbsp soy sauce

1 tsp cornflour (cornstarch)

1 tbsp sesame oil

125 g/4½ oz French beans, cut into 4 cm/ 1½ inch lengths

1 x 225 g/8 oz can bamboo shoots

salt and pepper

COOK'S TIP

Be sure to drain and rinse the beans before using, as they are usually canned in salty water, which will spoil the flavour of the finished dish.

1 Drain all the beans, rinse under cold water and drain again very thoroughly.

2 Cut 4 spring onions (scallions) into narrow slanting slices. Thinly slice the remainder and reserve for garnish.

3 Combine the pineapple and juice, ginger and syrup, lime rind and juice, soy sauce and cornflour (cornstarch) in a bowl.

4 Heat the oil in the wok, swirling it around until really hot. Add the spring onions (scallions) and stir-fry for about a minute, then add the French beans. Drain and thinly slice the bamboo shoots, add to the pan and continue to stir-fry for 2 minutes.

5 Add the pineapple and ginger mixture and bring just to the boil. Add the canned beans and stir until very hot – for about a minute.

6 Season to taste, sprinkled with the reserved chopped spring onions (scallions); or serve as a vegetable accompaniment.

Green Bean Stir-Fry

These beans are simply cooked in a spicy, hot sauce for a tasty and very easy recipe.

NUTRITIONAL INFORMATION

Calories . . . . .86 Sugars 4g
Protein . . . . .2g Fat 6g
Carbohydrates . . . .6g Saturates 1g

 5 MINS   5 MINS

SERVES 4

I N G R E D I E N T S

450 g/1 lb thin green beans

2 fresh red chillies

2 tbsp peanut oil

½ tsp ground star anise

1 garlic clove, crushed

2 tbsp light soy sauce

2 tsp clear honey

½ tsp sesame oil

1 Using a sharp knife, cut the green beans in half.

2 Slice the fresh chillies, removing the seeds first if you prefer a milder dish.

3 Heat the oil in a preheated wok or large frying pan (skillet) until the oil is almost smoking.

4 Lower the heat slightly, add the halved green beans to the wok and stir-fry for 1 minute.

5 Add the sliced red chillies, star anise and garlic to the wok and stir-fry for a further 30 seconds.

6 Mix together the soy sauce, honey and sesame oil in a small bowl.

7 Stir the sauce mixture into the wok. Cook for 2 minutes, tossing the beans to ensure that they are thoroughly coated in the sauce.

8 Transfer the mixture in the wok or pan to a warm serving dish and serve immediately.

VARIATION

This recipe is surprisingly delicious made with Brussels sprouts instead of green beans. Trim the sprouts, then shred them finely. Stir-fry the sprouts in hot oil for 2 minutes, then proceed with the recipe from step 4.

Pak Choi with Cashew Nuts

Plum sauce is readily available in jars and has a terrific, sweet flavour which complements the vegetables.

NUTRITIONAL INFORMATION

Calories . . . . .241 Sugars 7g
Protein . . . . .7g Fat 19g
Carbohydrate . . . .11g Saturates 4g

 5 MINS   15 MINS

SERVES 4

I N G R E D I E N T S

2 red onions

175 g/6 oz red cabbage

2 tbsp groundnut oil

225 g/8 oz pak choi

2 tbsp plum sauce

100 g/3½ oz/⅓ cup roasted cashew nuts

1 Using a sharp knife, cut the red onions into thin wedges and thinly shred the red cabbage.

2 Heat the groundnut oil in a large preheated wok or heavy-based frying pan (skillet) until the oil is really hot.

3 Add the onion wedges to the wok or frying pan (skillet) and stir-fry for about 5 minutes or until the onions are just beginning to brown.

4 Add the red cabbage to the wok and stir-fry for a further 2–3 minutes.

5 Add the pak choi leaves to the wok or frying pan (skillet) and stir-fry for about 5 minutes, or until the leaves have just wilted.

6 Drizzle the plum sauce over the vegetables, toss together until well combined and heat until the liquid is bubbling.

7 Scatter with the roasted cashew nuts and transfer to warm serving bowls.

VARIATION

Use unsalted peanuts instead of the cashew nuts, if you prefer.

Bamboo with Cucumber

A simple stir-fried side dish of canned bamboo shoots and sliced cucumber is the perfect accompaniment to a Chinese main meal.

NUTRITIONAL INFORMATION

Calories	101	Sugars	.......0.2g
Protein	.........3g	Fat	...........7g
Carbohydrate	....7g	Saturates	.......1g

 20 MINS   10 MINS

SERVES 4

INGREDIENTS

½ cucumber

2 tbsp sesame oil

4 shallots, chopped finely

1 garlic clove, sliced finely

350 g/12 oz can of bamboo shoots, drained

1 tbsp dry sherry

1 tbsp soy sauce

2 tsp cornflour (cornstarch)

1 tsp sesame seeds

salt

TO GARNISH

2 red chilli flowers (see page 15)

sliced spring onions (scallions)

1 Slice the cucumber thinly and sprinkle with salt. Leave for 10–15 minutes, then rinse with cold water. Prepare the chilli and spring onion (scallion) garnish.

2 Heat the sesame oil in a wok or frying pan (skillet) and add the shallots and garlic. Stir-fry for 2 minutes, until golden.

3 Add the bamboo shoots and cucumber to the wok or frying pan (skillet) and stir-fry for 2–3 minutes.

4 Blend together the dry sherry, soy sauce and cornflour (cornstarch). Add

to the bamboo shoots and cucumber, stirring to combine.

5 Cook for 1–2 minutes to thicken slightly, then add the sesame seeds and stir through.

6 Transfer the vegetables to a warmed serving dish. Garnish with the chilli flowers and chopped spring onion (scallion). Serve at once.

COOK'S TIP

Salting the cucumber before it is stir-fried draws out some of its moisture so that it stays crisp.

Add some very finely sliced carrot to this dish to add some extra colour, if you like.

Thai-Style Stir-Fried Noodles

This dish is considered the Thai national dish, as it is made and eaten everywhere – a one-dish, fast food for eating on the move.

NUTRITIONAL INFORMATION

Calories 407   Sugars 11g
Protein . . . . .14g   Fat 16g
Carbohydrate . . .56g   Saturates 3g

15 MINS   5 MINS

SERVES 4

I N G R E D I E N T S

225 g/8 oz dried rice noodles

2 red chillies, seeded and
   finely chopped

2 shallots, finely chopped

2 tbsp sugar

2 tbsp tamarind water

1 tbsp lime juice

2 tbsp light soy sauce

1 tbsp sunflower oil

1 tsp sesame oil

175 g/6 oz/¾ cup diced smoked tofu
   (bean curd)

pepper

2 tbsp chopped roasted peanuts,
   to garnish

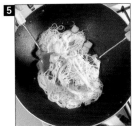

1 Cook the rice noodles as directed on the pack, or soak them in boiling water for 5 minutes.

2 Grind together the chillies, shallots, sugar, tamarind water, lime juice, light soy sauce and pepper to taste.

3 Heat both the oils together in a preheated wok or large, heavy frying pan (skillet) over a high heat. Add the tofu (bean curd) and stir for 1 minute.

4 Add the chilli mixture, bring to the boil, and cook, stirring constantly, for about 2 minutes, until thickened.

5 Drain the rice noodles and add them to the chilli mixture. Use 2 spoons to lift and stir them until they are no longer steaming. Serve immediately, garnished with the peanuts.

COOK'S TIP

This is a quick one-dish meal that is very useful if you are catering for a single vegetarian in the family.

Stir-Fried Bean Sprouts

Be sure to use fresh bean sprouts, rather than the canned variety, for this crunchy-textured dish.

NUTRITIONAL INFORMATION

Calories	98	Sugars	.........2g
Protein	.........2g	Fat	...........9g
Carbohydrate	....3g	Saturates	.......1g

5 MINS   5 MINS

SERVES 4

INGREDIENTS

250 g/9 oz fresh bean sprouts

2–3 spring onions (scallions)

1 medium red chilli pepper (optional)

3 tbsp vegetable oil

½ tsp salt

½ tsp sugar

1 tbsp light soy sauce

a few drops sesame oil (optional)

1 Rinse the bean sprouts in cold water, discarding any husks or small pieces that float to the top.

2 Drain the bean sprouts well on kitchen paper (paper towels).

COOK'S TIP

The red chilli pepper gives a bite to this dish – leave the seeds in for an even hotter taste. If you prefer a milder, sweeter flavour use red (bell) pepper instead of the chilli pepper. Core, seed and cut into strips in the same way.

3 Using a sharp knife, cut the spring onions (scallions) into short sections.

4 Thinly shred the red chilli pepper, if using, discarding the seeds.

5 Heat the vegetable oil in a preheated wok, swirling the oil around the base of the wok until it is really hot.

6 Add the bean sprouts, spring onions (scallions) and chilli pepper, if using, to the wok and stir-fry the mixture for about 2 minutes.

7 Add the salt, sugar, soy sauce and sesame oil, if using, to the mixture in the wok. Stir well to blend. Serve the bean sprouts hot or cold.

Cantonese Garden Vegetables

This dish tastes as fresh as it looks. Try to get hold of baby vegetables as they look and taste so much better in this dish.

NUTRITIONAL INFORMATION

Calories 130	Sugars 8g	
Protein 6g	Fat 8g	
Carbohydrate 8g	Saturates 1g	

 5 MINS 10 MINS

SERVES 4

INGREDIENTS

2 tbsp peanut oil

1 tsp Chinese five-spice powder

75 g/2¾ oz baby carrots, halved

2 celery sticks, sliced

2 baby leeks, sliced

50 g/1¾ oz mangetout (snow peas)

4 baby courgettes (zucchini), halved lengthwise

8 baby corn cobs

225 g/8 oz firm marinated tofu (bean curd), cubed

4 tbsp fresh orange juice

1 tbsp clear honey

celery leaves and orange zest, to garnish

cooked rice or noodles, to serve

VARIATION

Lemon juice would be just as delicious as the orange juice in this recipe, but use 3 tablespoons instead of 4 tablespoons.

1 Heat the peanut oil in a preheated wok or large frying pan (skillet) until almost smoking.

2 Add the Chinese five-spice powder, carrots, celery, leeks, mangetout (snow peas), courgettes (zucchini) and corn cobs and stir-fry for 3–4 minutes.

3 Add the tofu (bean curd) to the wok or frying pan (skillet) and cook for a further 2 minutes, stirring gently so the tofu (bean curd) does not break up.

4 Stir the fresh orange juice and clear honey into the wok or frying pan (skillet), reduce the heat and cook for 1–2 minutes.

5 Transfer the stir-fry to a serving dish, garnish with celery leaves and orange zest and serve with rice or noodles.

Stir-Fried Greens

Eat your greens in this most delicious way – stir-fried so that they retain their colour, crunch and flavour.

NUTRITIONAL INFORMATION

Calories	116	Sugars	. . . . .3g
Protein	. . . . .5g	Fat	. . . . .9g
Carbohydrate	. . . .5g	Saturates	. . . . . . .1g

5 MINS   10 MINS

SERVES 4

INGREDIENTS

8 spring onions (scallions)

2 celery sticks

125 g/4½ oz white radish (mooli)

125 g/4½ oz sugar snap peas or mangetout (snow peas)

175 g/6 oz Chinese leaves (cabbage)

175 g/6 oz bok choy or spinach

2 tbsp vegetable oil

1 tbsp sesame oil

2 garlic cloves, chopped finely

1 tbsp fish sauce

2 tbsp oyster sauce

1 tsp finely grated fresh ginger root

pepper

1 Slice the spring onions (scallions) and celery finely. Cut the white radish (mooli) into matchstick strips. Trim the sugar snap peas or mangetout (snow peas). Shred the Chinese leaves (cabbage) and shred the bok choy or spinach.

2 Heat the vegetable oil and sesame oil together in a wok or large frying pan (skillet). Add the garlic and fry for about 1 minute.

3 Add the spring onions (scallions), celery, white radish (mooli) and sugar snap peas or mangetout (snow peas) to the wok or frying pan (skillet) and stir-fry for about 2 minutes.

4 Add the Chinese leaves (cabbage) and bok choy or spinach. Stir-fry for about 1 minute.

5 Stir the fish sauce and oyster sauce into the vegetables with the grated ginger. Cook for 1 minute. Season with pepper to taste, transfer to a warm serving dish and serve at once.

VARIATION

Any variety – and any amount – of fresh vegetables can be used in this dish. Just make sure that harder vegetables, such as carrots, are cut very finely so that they cook quickly.

Use light soy sauce as an alternative to the fish sauce, if you prefer.

Eight Jewel Vegetables

This recipe, as the title suggests, is a colourful mixture of eight vegetables, cooked in a black bean and soy sauce.

NUTRITIONAL INFORMATION

Calories 110   Sugars 3g
Protein . . . . .4g   Fat 8g
Carbohydrate . . . .7g   Saturates 1g

5 MINS   10 MINS

SERVES 4

INGREDIENTS

2 tbsp peanut oil

6 spring onions (scallions), sliced

3 garlic cloves, crushed

1 green (bell) pepper, seeded
   and diced

1 red (bell) pepper, seeded and diced

1 fresh red chilli, sliced

2 tbsp chopped water chestnuts

1 courgette (zucchini), chopped

125 g/4½ oz oyster mushrooms

3 tbsp black bean sauce

2 tsp Chinese rice wine or dry sherry

4 tbsp dark soy sauce

1 tsp dark brown sugar

2 tbsp water

1 tsp sesame oil

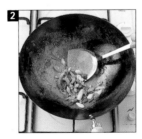  

1 Heat the peanut oil in a preheated wok or large frying pan (skillet) until it is almost smoking.

2 Lower the heat slightly, add the spring onions (scallions) and garlic and stir-fry for about 30 seconds.

3 Add the red and green (bell) peppers, fresh red chilli, water chestnuts and courgette (zucchini) to the wok or frying pan (skillet) and stir-fry for 2–3 minutes, or until the vegetables are just beginning to soften.

4 Add the oyster mushrooms, black bean sauce, Chinese rice wine or dry sherry, dark soy sauce, dark brown sugar and water to the wok and stir-fry for a further 4 minutes.

5 Sprinkle the stir-fry with sesame oil and serve immediately.

COOK'S TIP

Eight jewels or treasures form a traditional part of the Chinese New Year celebrations, which start in the last week of the old year. The Kitchen God, an important figure, is sent to give a report to heaven, returning on New Year's Eve in time for the feasting.

This is a Parragon Book
This edition published in 2002

Parragon
Queen Street House
4 Queen Street
Bath BA1 1HE, UK

ISBN: 0-75257-542-2

Printed in China

NOTE

This book uses metric and imperial measurements. Follow the same units of
measurement throughout; do not mix metric and imperial. All spoon measurements
are level: teaspoons are assumed to be 5 ml and tablespoons are assumed to be 15 ml.
Unless otherwise stated, milk is assumed to be full fat, eggs and individual vegetables
such as potatoes are medium and pepper is freshly ground black pepper.

The nutritional information provided for each recipe is per serving or per person.
Optional ingredients, variations or serving suggestions have not been included in the
calculations. The times given for each recipe are an approximate guide only because
the preparation times may differ according to the techniques used by different
people and the cooking times may vary as a result of the type of oven used.

Recipes using raw or very lightly cooked eggs should be
avoided by infants, the elderly, pregnant women, convalescents
and anyone suffering from an illness.